IMAGES
of America

KING ARTHUR
FLOUR COMPANY

IMAGES
of America

KING ARTHUR
FLOUR COMPANY

David A. Anderson
Foreword by Frank Sands

ARCADIA
PUBLISHING

Published by Arcadia Publishing
Charleston, South Carolina

Library of Congress Catalog Card Number: 2004104903

For all general information contact Arcadia Publishing at:
Telephone 843-853-2070
Fax 843-853-0044
E-mail sales@arcadiapublishing.com
For customer service and orders:
Toll-Free 1-888-313-2665

Visit us on the Internet at www.arcadiapublishing.com

*To those who have worked since 1790 to make
the King Arthur Flour Company what it is today.*

*And to Julia Child for her baking passion
and for bringing us all together in the kitchen.*

CONTENTS

FOREWORD

It is remarkable for a company to remain viable for more than two centuries—surviving wars and depressions and reacting to boom times as well as changing trends and competition often from very large and powerful companies. From what I personally know of the company for more than half of its lifetime, I would say that it has been led by honest, fair, competitive, and creative individuals whose guiding principles can be boiled down to "doing the right thing" in terms of product, people, trade practices, and relationship to the larger community.

For product, best epitomized by our King Arthur Flour, the commitment has always been to the very best quality (more costly chemical-free flour), placing price as a secondary factor. This has always been a challenge when so much of the food business is price-oriented. But, fortuitously, it has forced us to justify our price to our customers by explaining the stringent high quality, better performance, health and nutrition, and ultimately value that is inherent in our good King Arthur Flour. I can tell you from personal experience that, even though it has not been easy, it is a pleasure to be so closely associated with a product that is held in such high esteem by many thousands of home bakers and by many of the finest artisan bakers in the world. To be connected with a product that is widely known as the finest of its kind is extremely energizing and rewarding for me and for all the employee owners of the King Arthur Flour Company.

Perhaps that is one of the key factors in attracting such strongly committed, high-caliber people to the King Arthur Flour Company. We are all passionately proud of our flour and what we do in association with it. There is an inherent magic in being associated with the very best. So King Arthur Flour Company employees, even before they became owners, have acted like owners—committed, dependable, enthusiastic, creative, and attentive to our customers. Our recent expansion into *The Baker's Catalogue*, a retail store, an artisan bakery, and a baking education center is an example of this. It is rewarding and inspiring to know that, like our good King Arthur Flour, our fellow employee owners are the best in the business. And, of course, employee ownership is the ultimate expression of that feeling.

The King Arthur Flour Company's commitment to its business has naturally spread out into its trade, associating with bakers, flour distributors, millers, and vendors for the betterment of all. Many of us have assumed leading roles in these groups. This approach entails a great deal of extra time but is an expression of our commitment to a business and trade we love and respect. We appreciate the importance of supporting it.

Similarly, the King Arthur Flour Company has always had a sense of responsibility to its community. Having been an active part of the development of the free-enterprise system in the United States for more than 200 years, the King Arthur Flour Company and its employee-owners as individuals believe in, and participate in, the responsibility of business to support its community.

All in all, it has been and continues to be a meaningful and rewarding trip.

—Frank Sands
August 2004

INTRODUCTION

Imagine the United States in 1790. On January 4, Pres. George Washington delivered the first State of the Union address. On February 1, the U.S. Supreme Court convened for the first time. On March 22, Thomas Jefferson became the first U.S. secretary of state. Future U.S. presidents John Tyler (the 10th) and James Buchanan (the 15th) were just born, on March 29 in Charles City County, Virginia, and April 23 in Franklin County, Pennsylvania, respectively. On July 10, the House of Representatives voted to locate the national capital on a 10-square-mile site along the Potomac, and President Washington chose the exact location.

Also in 1790, a man named Henry Wood imported flour from England to Boston's Long Wharf and started today's King Arthur Flour Company. Perhaps Wood took note of the August 1, 1790, compilation by the new U.S. Census Bureau. It showed a population of 3,939,326 located in 16 states and the Ohio territory. Certainly, flour would be needed and wanted in this newly formed republic.

Actually, Wood's flour was so much in demand that he soon took on a partner and formed Henry Wood & Company. The years went by, and as the nation grew and thrived, so did their flour business.

In 1853, Henry Wood & Company purchased a large structure at 13 Long Wharf in Boston Harbor. The company was now smack-dab in one of the busiest ports in the world; there were 63 wharfs in Boston and 14 in neighboring Charlestown.

Boston boomed and grew its land mass by filling in the harbor around the wharves. In 1862, Henry Wood & Company was landlocked and, despite not moving at all, received a new address: 172 State Street.

In 1895, with more people involved, the company took a new name: Sands, Taylor & Wood. During the 1890s, a new milling technique developed in Hungary, enabling large amounts of wheat to be ground into white flour quickly. Competition grew in the flour business. Many new people jumped into the milling business, and the consistency and quality of flour became unpredictable. Sands, Taylor & Wood decided to carve a marketing niche as the company that distributed the finest-quality flour available anywhere.

This new flour, milled from a unique blend of 100 percent hard wheat with no additives, needed to enhance its baking qualities or its appearance. George Wood, one of the partners at that time but (not related to original founder Henry Wood) was inspired while in the audience of a Boston musical based on King Arthur and the Knights of the Round Table. Wood witnessed the same values in Arthurian legend he saw in his new exceptional flour: purity, loyalty, honesty, superior strength, and a dedication to a higher purpose. King Arthur Flour was introduced at the Boston Food Fair on September 10, 1896, and it became an immediate success.

ACKNOWLEDGMENTS

Many, many thanks to the Boston Public Library, Print Department; the Bostonian Society; the King Arthur Flour Company; Whitney Sands; and Frank and Brinna Sands for allowing me to dig through their respective collections of historic images and documents. Many, many thanks also to the employee owners of the King Arthur Flour Company; their passion for this great company is truly impressive. Also, a special thank-you to Brenda Hickory, who spent countless hours at her computer scanning and preparing for printing the many images in this book.

One

THE EARLY DAYS

From the 26th-floor open-air observation deck of the Custom House—a towering structure that Walt Whitman once called "the noblest form of commercial architecture in the world"— Boston rolls out below for miles. It was here that the more than 200-year history of the King Arthur Flour Company began.

To the north are more buildings than one can count, most in matching red brick. Shiny traffic snakes this way and that along the Leonard P. Zakim Bunker Hill Bridge, its two tallest points poking into the sky like replicas of the Bunker Hill Monument, located to the right, and four lanes extend in each direction under towering white strands. The Fleet Center, to the left, features a massive Boston Bruins' billboard with two words: "Wicked Intense." Moving right, over traffic, a Red Sox billboard atop a North End brick structure begs, "Keep the Faith." Closer, hugging Interstate 93, are Big Dig sandy construction areas.

Put aside the traffic, the new bridge, the Fleet Center, the billboards, and the construction, and historic Boston appears. The thin white spire of the Old North Church can be seen in the distance at two o'clock. Below, throngs of tiny pedestrians walk the ubiquitous red brick in and out of shadows around Faneuil Hall, where in 1772, Samuel Adams first spoke of the colonies uniting against the British.

To the east, down State Street is the end of Long Wharf. Today, white taxis wait in front of the Long Wharf Marriot, and on the water, a dozen clean white sailboats bob and rest. This stretch, from the Custom House down State Street to the water, is where the King Arthur Flour Company started in 1790. Its offices were here until 1922, when the company moved to Somerville, Massachusetts. State Street was not here at the start; it was water. The Custom House opened in 1847 so ships could sail to the eastern stairs of the building and have a tariff levied on their cargo. That was 57 years after Henry Wood starting importing flour down Long Wharf.

In 1853, George Cook and Henry Wood (ironically, not related to the original founder, Henry Wood) bought property down the street from the Custom House at 13 Long Wharf. As Boston's population grew and Long Wharf was filled in, this address became 172 State Street. The company moved into this Custom House tower at 131 State Street on February 6, 1904.

Today, there are not any reminders of the King Arthur Flour Company at 172 State Street, just traffic racing past concrete buildings. However, there are surviving images of this company in Boston, which are featured in the following pages.

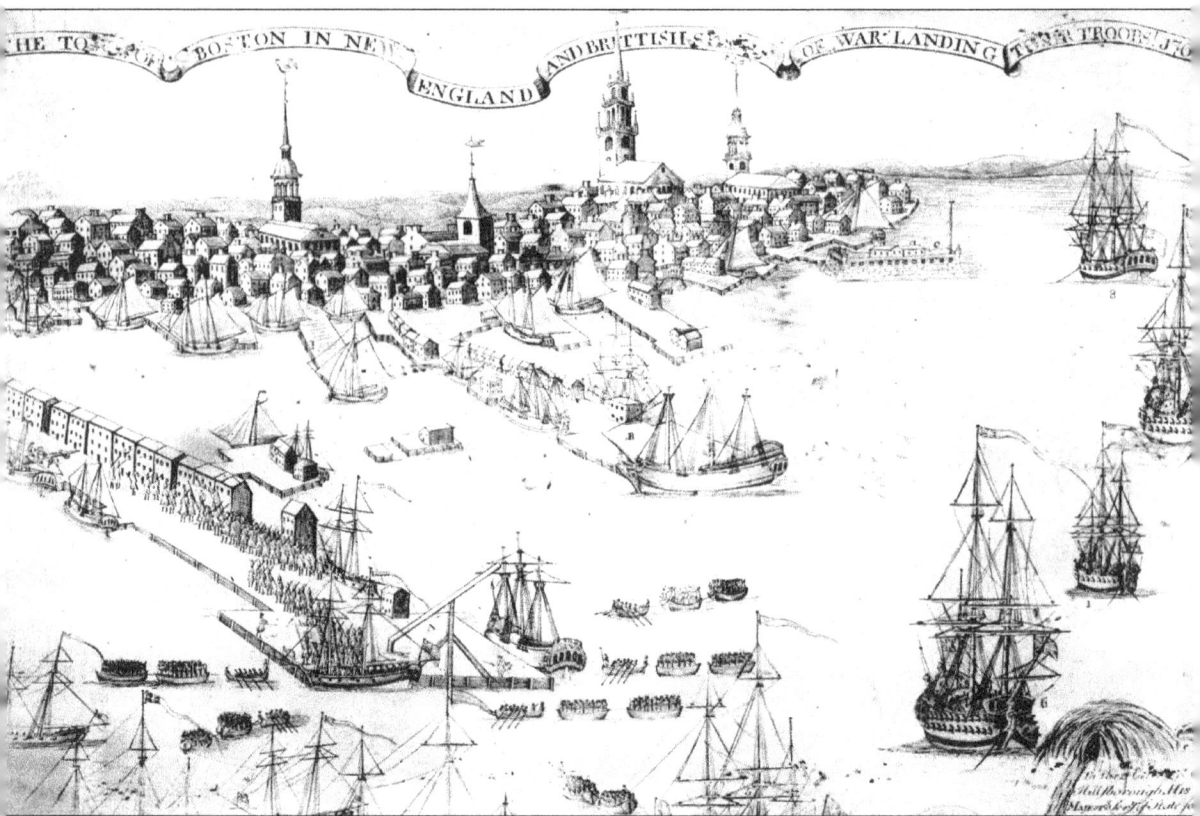

This engraving by Paul Revere shows British troops landing on Boston's Long Wharf in 1768. In March 1776, British general Sir William Howe and 1,100 loyalists retreated from Boston, also via Long Wharf. Just 14 years later, in this same location, sailing ships from England unloaded flour to start what is now the King Arthur Flour Company, the first flour company in America and the oldest food company in New England. (Courtesy of the Boston Public Library, Print Department.)

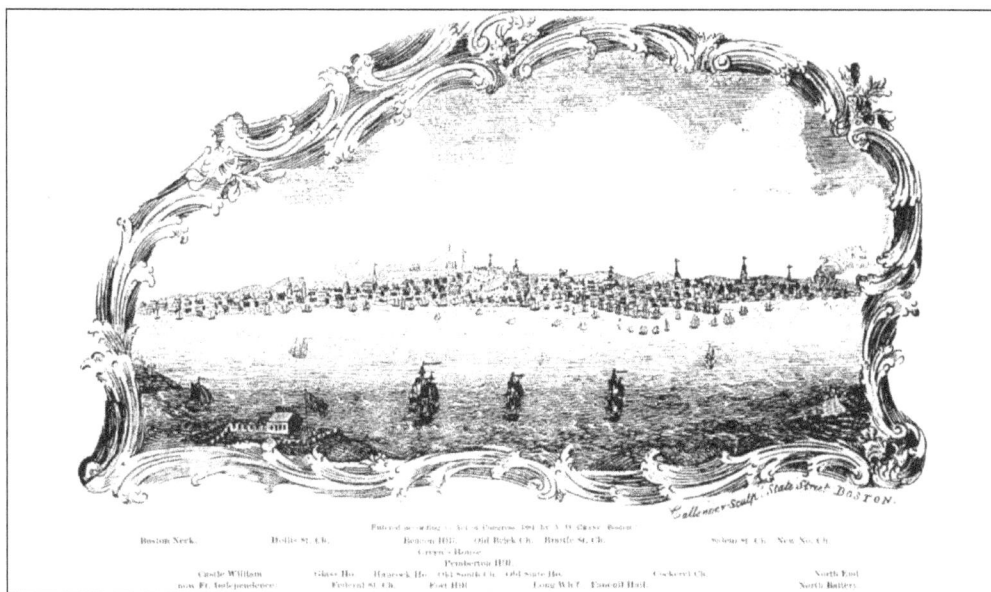

This view of Boston was drawn in 1788, just two years before Henry Wood started importing flour to Long Wharf for the beginning of today's King Arthur Flour Company. Long Wharf (right of center) was Boston's longest wharf, advancing nearly 2,000 feet into the sea and wide enough for stores and shops. This photographic reproduction of the original engraving was made in 1884. (Courtesy of the Boston Public Library, Print Department.)

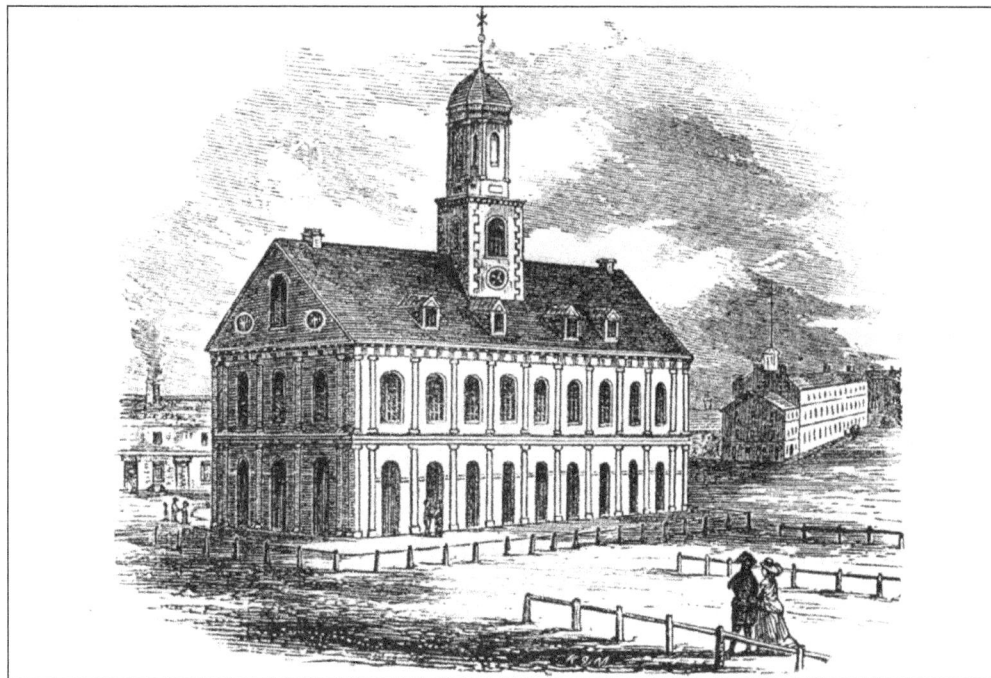

This etching of Boston's Faneuil Hall shows how this historic structure looked before its enlargement in 1805, 15 years after Henry Wood started what is now the King Arthur Flour Company a short walk away on Long Wharf. The identity of the etching's creator is unknown. (Courtesy of the Bostonian Society, Old State House.)

This 1833 photogravure of Robert Salmon's oil painting of Boston's Long and Central Wharves depicts the bustling shipping activity of the time. The offices of what is now the King Arthur Flour Company were on Long Wharf then and received flour brought from England on sailing ships. Robert Salmon immigrated to America from England in June 1828. He arrived in New York in July and spent a few months there before leaving for Boston in 1829. Boston harbor, at this time, was in its heyday, and Salmon achieved great success and became one of its greatest maritime artists. He remained in Boston until c.1841, at which time he returned to England. (Courtesy of the Boston Public Library, Print Department.)

This rare *c*. 1855 photograph of Boston's Long Wharf offers a street-level view looking northeast toward Atlantic Avenue. Signs for fish and grain merchants are affixed above store entryways on the cobblestone wharf. The company, at this time, was called Henry Wood & Company and was located at 13 Long Wharf. The Long Wharf addresses in this photograph are most likely between 35 and 42. While the flour sign cannot specifically be tied to what is now the King Arthur Flour Company, this photograph provides a glimpse of the area where the company operated. (Courtesy of the Bostonian Society, Old State House.)

Benjamin Franklin Sands, the oldest son of John Low Sands, was 15 years old in 1855, when he started working for Henry Wood & Company on Boston's Long Wharf. He eventually became part owner, and the company name changed to Sands & Fernald in 1878. He died on February 5, 1881, at the young age of 41, only six months after the death of his father.

Boston's Long Wharf is pictured in an E. W. Goodrich lantern slide dated *c.* 1860. The company name at this time was Henry Wood & Company, located at 13 Long Wharf. (Courtesy of the Bostonian Society, Old State House.)

This elevated view of State Street looking west to southwest is a photomechanical print dated c.1895, one year before King Arthur Flour was introduced at the Boston Food Fair. From this vantage point, company offices are on the right side of State Street behind the photographer. The company name changed to Sands, Taylor & Wood in 1895 and remained until it was officially renamed the King Arthur Flour Company in 1999. (Courtesy of the Bostonian Society, Old State House.)

This c. 1865 view of State Street looks east to northeast from the Old State House. The company name at this time was James Edmund & Company, located at 172 State Street (lower left). (Courtesy of the Bostonian Society, Old State House.)

15

Orin E. Sands, younger brother of Benjamin F. Sands, started working for the company at age 15 in 1865. By the age of 18, he was on the road; his territory spanned from New Hampshire down to Cape Cod. Orin took over leadership of the company when Benjamin passed away at age 41 in 1881. Orin Street in Cambridge is named after him.

Mark Crosby Taylor (July 17, 1850–June 28, 1924) grew up in the town of Orleans on Cape Cod. He moved to Boston and joined the flour company in July 1874. He started as bookkeeper and, in 1885, became a partner. The name of the firm then became Sands, Sprauge & Taylor.

In 1878, the name of the company was Sands & Fernald, after Benjamin Franklin Sands and Charles W. Fernald. This early photograph shows the offices, at that time, on Boston's Long Wharf. The company went through 10 name changes from 1830 until 1895, when the name changed to Sands, Taylor & Wood. It was not until 1999 that the next name changed to the King Arthur Flour Company, in honor of the company's signature flour.

Boston's Custom House, pictured c. 1885, opened in 1847 and played a major role in the history of the King Arthur Flour Company. Sailing ships would arrive at Long Wharf with flour and dock at the base of the Custom House to pay tariffs. As the harbor around Long Wharf was filled in, the offices of Sands, Taylor & Wood changed from 13 Long Wharf (also referred to at the time as 13 Boston Pier) to 172 State Street, without physically moving at all. In 1904, Sands, Taylor & Wood moved up the street to the Custom House at 131 State Street. Today, the Custom House serves as a hotel. (Courtesy of the Boston Public Library, Print Department.)

George E. Wood joined the flour company in 1889. On January 2, 1895, it became Sands, Taylor & Wood, the final title of the firm for almost 100 years until the name changed to that of its signature product and became today's King Arthur Flour Company.

In 1896, Mark Taylor, Orin Sands, and George Wood (pictured from left to right) of the Sands, Taylor & Wood Company introduced their new and exceptional product: King Arthur Flour. This new flour was milled from a unique blend of 100 percent hard wheat with no additives needed to enhance its baking qualities or appearance. Wood received inspiration for the name while in the audience of a Boston musical based on King Arthur and the Knights of the Round Table. He witnessed the same values in Arthurian legend he saw in his new exceptional flour: purity, loyalty, honesty, superior strength, and a dedication to a higher purpose. King Arthur Flour was introduced at the Boston Food Fair on September 10, 1896, and it became an immediate success.

The artwork created to announce King Arthur Flour in 1896 was used in the company's advertising for years, and as a result, it is immediately recognizable on all of the company's products today.

After King Arthur Flour was launched by the Sands, Taylor & Wood Company in 1896, it became an immediate great success. Its emblem is as popular today as it was during the late 1800s, when it could be seen on barrels in horse-drawn wagons. Each barrel weighed 196 pounds, or 14 English stones. Additional barrelheads featuring the logo were hung below the carriage for added exposure.

21

Frank Edgar Sands, the oldest son of Benjamin Franklin and Mary Mayberry Sands, began working for Sands, Taylor & Wood in 1896 at the age of 31. The King Arthur Flour brand was created in his initial year with the company, and his first duties included development, sales, and marketing. In 1917, Sands became president of the company after his uncle, Orin Sands, passed away. He remained president until his death in 1943.

Two

THE 20TH CENTURY

The 20th century started with horse-drawn carriages and advanced to space travel. Through the Great Depression and World Wars I and II, the King Arthur brand endured. In addition to flour, King Arthur, for a while, also produced coffee and tea, biscuit mix, wheat germ, farin-o-germ, and cereal. These items were discontinued over time, but it is interesting to note that the company, through *The Baker's Catalogue*, reintroduced more than 100 baking mixes at the end of the century, and in 2003, started again selling all-natural quick mixes in stores.

At the start of the 20th century, King Arthur Flour had only been available four years, and the company offices were still on Boston's Long Wharf. In 1986, after being headquartered in Massachusetts for its first 194 years, the company moved to Norwich, Vermont. In between, a great deal happened to shape the state of the company today.

This *c.* 1900 photograph features one of the wagons used to transport barrels of King Arthur Flour to customers. The office window of Sands, Taylor & Wood is in the background on the right, placing the location of this photograph at 172 State Street in Boston. The barrels were positioned on the wagons for maximum visibility of the popular King Arthur emblem, an early advertising effort similar to today's graphics on trucks. Note the chains on the rear wheels to provide traction through the dirt streets.

This c. 1900 photograph looks west up State Street from Atlantic Avenue. The offices of Sands, Taylor & Wood are on the right side of the street. (Courtesy of the Bostonian Society, Old State House.)

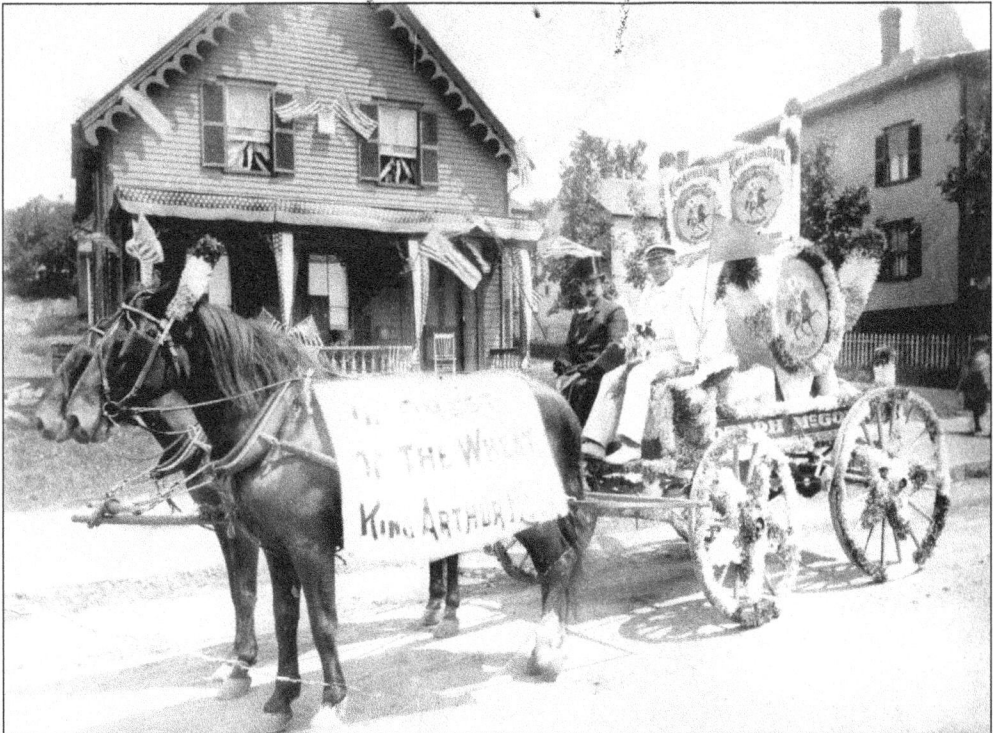

"The Finest of the Wheat, King Arthur Flour," reads the banner covering the horses of this buggy, which are dressed up for an Independence Day parade c. 1900. (Courtesy of the library of Clinton, Massachusetts.)

A King Arthur truck from the early 1900s features the popular logo and other company advertising.

In the early 1900s, the King Arthur Flour logo and related advertising were creatively used on buildings and public transportation throughout New England. Note the large circular billboard to the right of the railway car on the building's third floor that features the logo and knight on horseback. A smaller, partially obscured King Arthur Flour billboard is also on the first floor. This *c.* 1910 photograph shows a trolley of the Georgetown, Rowley & Ipswich Street Railway in Haverhill, Massachusetts. (Courtesy of the Boston Public Library, Print Department.)

A note on this photograph of Main Street in Gloucester, Massachusetts, reads, "Notice our (Sign)." The King Arthur Flour sign is on the right. This image was on a postcard sent from Gloucester to Baltimore in 1906 using a 1¢ stamp.

This ornate horse-drawn wagon from the turn of the century features the King Arthur Flour logo on each side and a young, happy girl alongside the driver.

Frank Edgar Sands is pictured in the offices of Sands, Taylor & Wood.

The company offices moved into the Custom House at 131 State Street in 1904. This July 1905 view looking east down Long Wharf was taken at or near the location of the company offices. The United Fruit Company is located on the south side of the wharf. The Dominion Atlantic Railway steamship line is in the center of the photograph. (Courtesy of the Bostonian Society, Old State House.)

This 1908 photograph by Thomas E. Marr shows Boston's lower State Street in a view looking toward the ferry terminal and waterfront. The photograph was probably taken from the area of the Custom House farther up State Street, where the company offices were then located. (Courtesy of the Boston Public Library, Print Department.)

31

This street-level view looking northwest of the Custom House tower, which is under construction *c.* 1913, shows the location of the Sands, Taylor & Wood offices. Several horse-drawn wagons fill McKinley Square. (Courtesy of the Bostonian Society, Old State House.)

This view from Boston Harbor in 1914 looks west of Long Wharf at the Custom House tower under construction. The offices of Sands, Taylor & Wood were in the Custom House at this time. (Courtesy of the Bostonian Society, Old State House.)

This photograph, taken *c.* 1916, shows the Custom House tower, which was just completed. The Board of Trade Building is located to the left, west of the Custom House. The rounded southwest elevation of the Flour Exchange Building, located at 177 Milk Street, is in the right corner. (Courtesy of the Bostonian Society, Old State House.)

This picture, taken in 1918, shows a vibrant market district and the Boston waterfront from the Custom House tower, where the company offices were at that time. The Custom House tower was built from 1913 to 1915 and, with 16 floors, became Boston's first skyscraper. The city had imposed height restrictions of only 125 feet until the Custom House was built. The flour company was located in the Custom House until it moved to Somerville, Massachusetts, in 1923. Long Wharf and State Street are farthest right in this photograph. (Courtesy of the Boston Public Library, Print Department.)

In the early 1920s, elaborate window displays were part of the creative King Arthur Flour marketing plan, as seen in this photograph from Charles & Company in New York City. Note the diorama in the middle of the display featuring a castle and knight figures. The inscription above the scene reads, "King Arthur Flour, America's Highest Grade Flour, Never Bleached."

Donald Phipps Sands (January 4, 1895–February 13, 1937) died at the young age of 42 of coronary thrombosis. Sands advanced the sales of King Arthur Flour in new markets, such as New York. He also attended Harvard, went to the Mexican border with Gen. John J. Pershing in pursuit of Pancho Villa, served as a first lieutenant with the Yankee Division during World War I, and refereed hockey in the 1932 Olympics in Lake Placid, New York.

Walter Edgar Sands, born on February 25, 1900, graduated from Dartmouth College in Hanover, New Hampshire, in 1922. He began working for his family's flour business in 1926, when the headquarters were in Somerville, Massachusetts. Sands was elected president of the company in 1944. After finishing at Dartmouth and before starting a long career with Sands, Taylor & Wood, he worked as an entertainer. He was in the musical comedy *Topsy and Eva* with the Duncan sisters and performed other vaudeville acts.

Walter Edgar Sands (third from the left), president of Sands, Taylor & Wood, is pictured on October 7, 1949.

The Sands, Taylor & Wood Company always proudly displayed mentions of King Arthur Flour and other products everywhere possible, including on company vehicles and on the roof of the Cambridge, Massachusetts, headquarters, as seen in this 1957 photograph. The large King Arthur sign could be seen from the adjacent Alewife Parkway and was illuminated in red to be highly visible at night.

At the American Institute of Baking in Chicago, Illinois, Frank E. Sands (fourth person down the table on right) participated in a baking class. The photograph was taken in January 1964. Sands had just started working for the company the year before, the fifth generation of the Sands family to do so.

Charles A. Bifano (left) with his father, Charles J. Bifano (center), receives the Sands Memorial Scholarship from Frank E. Sands, then vice president of the Sands, Taylor & Wood Company in this 1965 photograph. This $1,000 scholarship, created as a living memorial to the late Frank E. and Donald P. Sands, was awarded annually to the outstanding apprentice baker in New England. The Bifanos operated Crescent Home Bakery in Brockton and Randolph, Massachusetts. (Courtesy of the Boston Public Library, Print Department; photograph by Fay Foto Service.)

The 1966 Sands Memorial Scholarship winner was Louis Piantoni Jr. Pictured are, from left to right, Frank E. Sands, Piantoni, and Walter E. Sands.

This photograph in the *Lexington Minute-Man* newspaper shows Frank E. Sands presenting the $1,000 Sands Memorial Scholarship to Ronald Murray. To the right is Murray's employer, Robert Hopkins, of Brown's Bakery, in Everett, Massachusetts.

Gus Saunders (seated, left) ran the popular *Boston Kitchen* radio show on WNAC. Walter E. Sands is seated next to Saunders. Standing to the right is Frank E. Sands, then vice president of the company. The photograph was taken in 1966.

In 1967, the Wayside Inn gristmill in Sudbury, Massachusetts, was leased by the company to mill King Arthur whole-wheat flour. This mill was an exact reproduction of a water-driven gristmill built in 1928 by Henry Ford. It was also a tourist attraction open for daily tours and was located next to the Wayside Inn, made famous in *Tales of a Wayside Inn, by* Henry Wadsworth Longfellow.

Walter E. Sands (center) is pictured at the Wayside Inn gristmill in Sudbury, Massachusetts.

While attending Harvard Business School in 1963, Frank E. Sands II joined the Sands, Taylor & Wood Company, the fifth generation of the Sands family to do so. He became president in 1967. In 1984, he moved the company to its present location in Norwich, Vermont. His wife, Brinna Sands, wrote *The King Arthur Flour 200th Anniversary Cookbook* in 1990. Since then, the book has sold more than 100,000 copies and has become the cornerstone of many kitchen libraries. With her husband, Brinna founded *The Baker's Catalogue* and helped write *The Baker's Companion* cookbook, published in 2003. In 1996, with their children not looking to take over the company, Frank and Brinna (pictured in 1987) decided to make the employees the owners and initiated the Employee Stock Ownership Plan (ESOP).

Three

ADVERTISEMENTS AND PROMOTIONS

King Arthur Flour was introduced at the Boston Food Fair in October 1896. The company booth at the fair was designed like a castle, and promotion continued afterwards with a man dressed as King Arthur who roamed Boston's streets atop a black horse. An article from the *Boston Post*, on November 14, 1896, describes how "a horseman clad in glittering armor and armed cap-a-pie has been creating no small sensation of late as he guided his prancing steed through the streets. . . . The standard bears the legend 'King Arthur Flour,' and the inference is obvious—that King Arthur was a champion without fear and above reproach, so is King Arthur Flour the peerless champion of modern civilization. The idea and method of carrying it out are the cleverest advertising combination of the day."

The King Arthur Flour Company has continued to carry out creative advertising and promotions through the years up to the present. Whether it was driving a musical truck through the streets of New York in the 1920s; inserting in flour bags collectible national defense artwork during World War II; running humorous newspaper ads of King Arthur dealing with 1940s issues; or showcasing, toward the end of the 20th century, a passion for baking in the form of free classes across the United States, the King Arthur Flour Company has always found a fun way to get their message out.

Boston, Apl. 15th 1871

M. E. F. Fernald, Esq.

To PLUNKET & WALTERS, Dr.

MERCHANT TAILORS,

JOHN R. PLUNKET
R. F. WALTERS.

No. 18 BROADWAY, SOUTH BOSTON.

HO! ALL YE WITH FAMILIES!

Have you heard the News?

What News? Why, **B. FRANKLIN SANDS** is selling **FLOUR**, at the Corner of **Wyeth** and **Garden Streets**, at from **Twenty-five to Fifty Cents per barrel less** than it can be bought for elsewhere. Do you ask how he does it? It is this way:---Having facilities for purchasing of the receivers in large lots, at the lowest cash price, he is enabled to sell lower than those who are obliged to buy at second hand, viz., of the jobbers, who of course must have a profit as well as interest on their money, for they generally sell on time.

TERMS:

As I buy for Cash so I sell for Cash, and thus avoid making Purchasers pay for losses occasioned by bad debts.

N. B. Flour delivered in any part of the City free of expense, and if any barrel proves not to be what it is represented, the money will be refunded with the greatest pleasure. Also, all orders sent through the Post Office will meet with prompt attention.

Call and Try me once, and I have no fears for the future.

B. FRANKLIN SANDS.

E. L. MITCHELL, PRINTER, 43 COMMERCIAL STREET, BOSTON.

Two of the earliest advertisements were Benjamin Franklin Sands's first announcement of business in 1878, when the company name changed to Sands & Fernald, and a handbill signed by Benjamin Franklin Sands c. 1880.

THE "KING ARTHUR" STANDARD.

A horseman clad in glittering armor and armed cap-a-pie has been creating no small sensation of late as he guided his prancing steed through the streets of the Hub. No stranger contrast can well be imagined than this figure of medieval romance set down in the busy turmoil and traffic of modern Boston.

It seems at first sight that one of Walter Scott's heroes had come to life again; or, perchance, that a new Don Quixote had arisen to tilt against the deadly trolley.

The Crusaders' cross gleams on the coat of mail and adorns the silken standard that he bears aloft. It is, in truth, King Arthur come to earth again—the picture of that gallant warrior is literally perfect. The standard bears the legend "King Arthur Flour," and the inference is obvious—that as King Arthur was a champion without fear and above reproach, so is King Arthur Flour the peerless champion of modern civilization. The idea and the method of carrying it out are the cleverest advertising combination of the day.

Boston Post — Sunday Nov 14
— Kindly preserve —
97

A November 14, 1896, *Boston Post* article announces a man dressed as King Arthur riding a horse through the streets of Boston.

King Arthur Flour advertising artwork is pictured with the years to which each corresponds. Many of these messages are still a major part of the company's marketing message today.

 **The Foundation of Successful Cooking**

 **Makes Bread Light and White**

 **Makes Bread with Character**

Makes Good Bread Possible

Never Bleached That Means Everything

Makes More Loaves to the Barrel

Good Advice  **Use King Arthur**

Try a Bag  **Try a Barrel**

Good Cooks Like It  **Good Cooks Use It**

 **Stands at the Top of High Grade Flour**

 **Never Bleached Just Nature's Natural Flavor**

 **Made from the Finest Selected Wheat**

Proof from
Boston Evening Transcript

A company proof shows different advertising messages in the Boston *Evening Transcript*.

KING ARTHUR FLOUR

The most important things in a business are confidence in the integrity of the men who manage it and the merchandise offered its patrons. This business was built on honor by its founders and will so be maintained.

We seek Wider Knowledge, Greater Enthusiasm, More Friendliness.

SANDS, TAYLOR & WOOD CO.

This is one of the early window display ads for King Arthur Flour. Words such as "integrity" and "honor" have been important in describing the King Arthur brand from its beginning in 1896 up to the present.

TELEPHONE HAYMARKET NO 92

SANDS, TAYLOR & WOOD,

FLOUR

No. 172 State Street.

O E SANDS
M C TAYLOR
G E WOOD

BOSTON, MASS.

This three- by five-inch card was developed after the company name changed to Sands, Taylor & Wood, while it was still located at 172 State Street (originally 13 Long Wharf) from 1895 to 1904. The small print at the top reads, "Telephone Haymarket No. 92."

A barrel of King Arthur Flour was often given as a gift in turn-of-the-century New England. This 1912 postcard, reminding the recipient that King Arthur Flour by the barrel or half-barrel is "Sensible, Elegant, Valuable," was mailed with a 1¢ stamp.

WHAT BETTER GIFT?

A WHOLE OR HALF BARREL

King Arthur Flour

A Trim Package

Sensible - Elegant - Valuable

King Arthur Flour

AN UNBLEACHED FLOUR

Made from the finest selected wheat.
The kind of flour that makes the kind of bread that people like to eat.

PURE, WHOLESOME, PERFECTLY MILLED

Sands, Taylor & Wood Co.

131 State Street - - - - - Boston

An advertisement, while the company was located in the Boston Custom House at 131 State Street (1904–1923), communicates strong points about King Arthur Flour that are still important today: an unbleached flour, made from the finest selected wheat, pure, wholesome, perfectly milled, and certainly the kind of flour that makes the bread people like to eat.

This turn-of-the-century advertisement lists the barrel price for King Arthur Flour at $6 and the bag price at 80¢. Note the unique face and elaborate detail of King Arthur (left) with the setting sun and palm trees in the distance.

This 1913 advertisement from the company offices at 131 State Street in Boston lists King Arthur Flour prices ranging from $6.75 per barrel to 35¢ for 1/32 of a barrel sack.

This *c.* 1920 magazine advertisement offers a flour container "substantial in construction and beautiful in finish" for sale, including delivery at $2.50, the manufacturing cost. A flour sifter container from the early 1900s (below) is on display at Baker's Store in Norwich, Vermont. Flour was poured in at the top. Turning the handle allowed sifted flour to descend into the drawer at the bottom. Each container held 24.5 pounds or one-eighth of a barrel of King Arthur Flour.

Long before developing today's King Arthur whole-wheat flour (which, in 2004, became the best-selling whole-wheat flour in the United States), the company distributed Enright's whole-wheat flour when their offices were in Somerville, Massachusetts.

Before joining Sands, Taylor & Wood, Walter E. Sands worked as an entertainer. He used these musical skills for one of his first promotions of King Arthur Flour. In 1927, Sands outfitted a truck with a calliope (a keyboard instrument resembling an organ and consisting of a series of whistles surrounded by steam or compressed air) and a wooden carving of King Arthur Flour and drove through the streets of New York. On one of his initial trips, he was arrested in violation of an ordinance against playing music in New York's streets. After his plight was heard by Mayor Jimmy Walker, Sands was given an "itinerant music license" and was allowed to continue driving, playing music, and promoting King Arthur Flour around the city.

This c. 1928 photograph shows Walter E. Sands's King Arthur Flour musical truck in the Bronx.

This truck, used to promote King Arthur Flour in New York City in 1927, remained part of the company's marketing effort for several years. It visited new store openings and participated in parades.

The horse's head from Walter E. Sands's historic truck is on display at the King Arthur Flour Company's Norwich, Vermont, office.

The King Arthur Flour musical truck is pictured at a store opening in 1949.

For the Queen of the Kitchen!

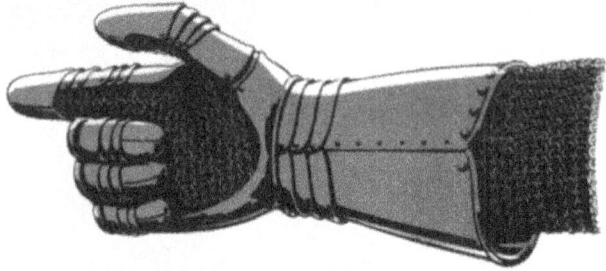

A WONDERFUL THING HAPPENS...
ON THE WAY TO YOUR STORE!

This early advertisement directed at the "Queen of the Kitchen" features the armored forearm and pointed index finger of King Arthur.

APPLY PASTE HERE
BE SURE AND PUT EACH PICTURE IN SPACE INDICATED IN ALBUM

BOYS AND GIRLS!!!

Don't miss a single picture. Pictures of our Marines, Army, Navy, Tanks, Airplanes, Submarines, etc. A picture in every bag of KING ARTHUR FLOUR. A postcard or letter will bring you free a beautiful album in which you can paste all your pictures, with a story of each picture. Send now as the supply is limited.

FREE FOR ALL THE LADIES

Illustrated Booklet "Primer of Bread Making" which shows in detail every step in bread making and also gives easy-to-make recipes for rolls, coffee ring, sweet doughs, and dough-nuts. Send name and address and we will mail at once. Send now as the supply is limited.

KING ARTHUR FLOUR
(NEW ENGLAND'S OLDEST FLOUR COMPANY)
SOMERVILLE P. O.   BOSTON, MASS.

During World War II, inserts in King Arthur Flour bags featured branches of the country's national defense. Collectors of the images sent postcards or letters to the company and received an album to paste them in.

58

DESTROYER

Shown here are the dramatically illustrated destroyer and army transport collectors' cards. In 1943, some 500,000 inserts were sent out in April, and another 500,000 had to be ordered in October due to the popularity of the program.

ARMY TRANSPORT

59

TANK

Shown are the tank and army searchlight collectors' cards. The World War II illustrations were done by Robert Russell. When the war images ran out, a new series of 24 bird images were developed as inserts. The bird series was painted by Jack Murray.

ARMY SEARCHLIGHT

In 1947, Marjorie Mills, billed as New England's foremost food expert, endorsed King Arthur Flour on Boston's WBZ radio. In nine months, 30,000 requests were received for *Primers of Bread Baking*, a record response at the time.

Paul Golub of Stop & Shop markets and Marjorie Mills are shown at the grand opening of a new Stop & Shop in Quincy, Massachusetts, c. 1947. The sign to the top left indicates the products on display were recommended by Mills. Note the two five-pound bags of King Arthur Flour located in the upper middle section of the display.

When Marjorie Mills made a store appearance in the late 1940s to promote King Arthur Flour and other items, large crowds were often there to greet her, as seen in this historic photograph taken in Cranston, Rhode Island.

Marjorie Mills and John Hulan appear at the Garden City store in Cranston, Rhode Island, c. 1947 in November to promote her display of products made popular on her radio broadcasts. Note the different-sized King Arthur Flour bags at the base of each table.

This series of clever and humorous advertisements, each wrapped in a border touting, "King Arthur," "All White," and "Never Bleached" repeatedly, ran in the *Boston Globe, Boston Herald*, and other New England newspapers in 1947.

It's the Shirt Shortage, I Suppose

All Purpose
King Arthur Flour

The theme throughout this series of advertisements is of King Arthur in 1940s Americana situations: talking on the phone, walking down the street in front of a well-dressed couple, sticking his head in a kitchen window to get some hot doughnuts, and riding his horse through a bed of petunias.

Get that Horse out of my Petunias!

All Purpose
King Arthur Flour

NOTHING BUT *Good Results* WITH

King Arthur

I never knew such bread or rolls,
And every day my family scolds
Because I never make enough
Of pies, and cakes, and bread and "stuff"
With good King Arthur.

But still, I really must complain,
My energy is on the wane;
They eat my baking up so fast
It doesn't get a chance to last —
That's good King Arthur!

*An unsolicited letter from
Mrs. T. A. W. — Massachusetts*

King Arthur *FOR GOOD RESULTS!*

Through the years, the King Arthur Flour Company has received vast numbers of wonderful letters. One, sent in the form of a poem, made it into this advertisement that featured not only King Arthur Flour but the company's tea, coffee, and biscuit mix. In 2004, the company returned to printing unsolicited letters, this time on the top of its flour packaging.

A promotion from when the company was headquartered in Cambridge, Massachusetts, offers a King Arthur pastry cloth and non-ravel rolling pin cover for only 50¢ with a coupon (regularly $1.50).

In 1964, radio advertising played a major role in the King Arthur Flour marketing plan. This promotional flyer for WBZ radio in Boston mentions that King Arthur Flour's message reaches "47,800 housewives in New England on the average quarter hour."

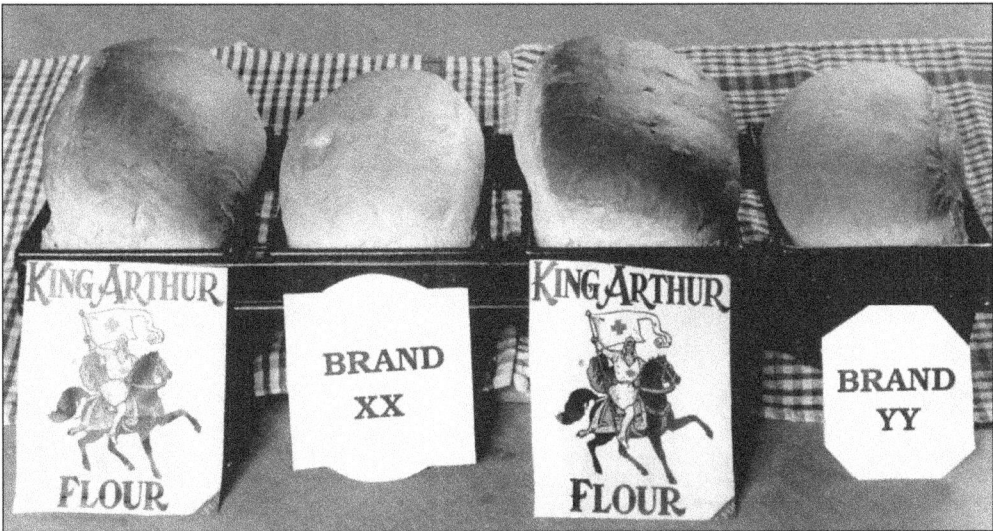

The superior baking attributes of King Arthur Flour compared to other popular flours can be seen in this promotional photograph. The high-quality hard wheat used to make King Arthur Flour contains more protein than other flours. As a result, King Arthur Flour contains more protein, too—as much as 20 percent more than ordinary American flours. Protein equals gluten, the magical elastic substance that makes bread rise.

Sifting was an advertising message as well. Because King Arthur Flour is (and always has been) pre-sifted 33 times, the only "sifting" required is with a spoon to a measuring cup.

A King Arthur Flour in-store promotion advertised on Boston's WBOS radio offered listeners a chance to "meet Queen Guinevere and receive a free Baker's Dozen recipe booklet."

Bleach belongs in bottles... not in flour!

KING ARTHUR FLOUR'S never bleached! How come it's so white?

First, King Arthur buys only hard Spring wheat . . . the most flavorful, nutritious, high-protein wheat grown. Sure, it's more expensive, but King Arthur believes in starting with the best. Instead of taking short cuts, and adding chemicals to bleach it, King Arthur patiently grinds and sifts its wheat 33 times. Then, only the choice, tender heart of the wheat berry remains . . . to give you the finest, *naturally* white flour you can buy.

People who do know the difference in flours . . . who care about quality, and take pride in their baking . . . find they get the best results with all-purpose, unbleached King Arthur Flour. With King Arthur you use *less* flour to do *more* baking . . . ⅛ cup less than called for in any bleached flour recipe. Try a bag today and you'll never use any other!

TRY THIS DELICIOUS "CAKE-PAN" CHOCOLATE CAKE

Mix it right in your baking pan — no bowls to wash. Makes one 8" cake.

1½ cups King Arthur Flour · 6 tablespoons cooking oil
1 cup sugar · (or melted shortening)
3 tablespoons unsweetened cocoa · 1 tablespoon vinegar
1 teaspoon soda · 1 teaspoon vanilla
½ teaspoon salt · 1 cup cold water

Set oven at 350 F. Put dry ingredients into sifter. Sift directly into ungreased cake pan (8" square). Make 3 holes in dry mixture. Pour cooking oil in first hole. Pour vinegar in second hole. Pour vanilla in third hole. Pour cold water over all. Stir with fork until evenly blended. Bake 35-40 minutes. Invert to cool and remove from pan, or frost right in pan.

SEND FOR **FREE** KING ARTHUR BOOK OF 13 QUICK 'N EASY RECIPES
KING ARTHUR FLOUR COMPANY
130 Fawcett St., Cambridge, Mass. 02138

Please send me your free recipe book, "Home Baker's Dozen."

NAME _____

ADDRESS _____

STATE _____ CITY _____

"King Arthur Flour's never bleached! How come it's so white?" asks this *c.* 1956 advertisement. Many flour companies use low-grade wheat and chemically bleach their flour to whiten it. Not only is this added bleach unhealthy (it is the same bleach used to wash clothes), but it strips nutrients from the flour. King Arthur Flour, because it starts with the highest quality wheat followed by a patient milling process, is never bleached, nor are chemicals of any kind added. "Then, only the choice, tender heart of the wheat berry remains . . . to give you the finest, naturally white flour you can buy."

A King Arthur Flour Company store display features five-pound bags for 99¢ apiece in May 1981. Pictured standing in the back are King Arthur Flour employees Bill O'Connor (second from left) and John Schwarz (right).

Only one brand of flour makes bread, week after week.

King Arthur Flour makes profit for *you*, week after week. Because it's the flour serious bakers prefer, week in and week out.

Why is King Arthur the preferred brand among heavy flour users? In a word, *quality.* It's our quality that keeps your customers coming back for King Arthur. It's our quality that commands a consistent selling price and produces good profits, all year long.

And it's our quality that's made King Arthur number one in dollar sales in the Boston/Providence market in 1984. In fact, sales of our two pound bags are up 90%. Sales of our five pound bags are up 20%. Sales of 10 and 25 pound bags have *doubled* the sales of 10 and 25 pound bags of the two leading national brands, *combined!*

In short, King Arthur is the *only* brand of flour in New England whose sales are growing.

Moreover, we're committed to keep them growing. We're spending more dollars on advertising and public relations than any other brand in New England.

Already, we've seen a terrific response to our promotional baking classes, which we co-sponsor with area supermarkets. Conducted by our baking specialist Michael Jubinsky, these classes have been excellent traffic builders, attracting overflow crowds.*

Featuring King Arthur Flour adds a prestigious image to your store. So when it comes to branded flour, make King Arthur your first choice. And enjoy your weekly bread.

King Arthur Flour
Treated with nothing but respect.

* To set up a promotional baking class, call Frank Sands at King Arthur Flour (802) 649-3881

This 1984 advertisement to the grocery retail trade communicates the financial advantages of carrying and selling King Arthur Flour. Distribution dramatically increased in the 1990s, as more and more people across the country asked their local grocer to carry King Arthur Flour. This advertisement also offers local supermarkets the chance to co-sponsor a new promotional baking class with Michael Jubinsky, the beginning of today's national baking class tours around the country.

In 200 years, we've never bleached, bromated nor conglomerated.

Two centuries ago, our only product was flour. It still is. And we're still the same independent company dedicated to producing the highest quality all-natural flour your customers can buy. The only difference is that now we're telling them about King Arthur with more advertising and PR support than all other brands combined. *Which helps to make King Arthur Flour the most profitable brand you can sell.* And that's another thing we have no intention of changing.

Since 1790
Quality products of Sands, Taylor & Wood Co.

King Arthur Flour
Treated with nothing but respect.

As part of the King Arthur Flour Company's 200th anniversary celebration, this ad ran in *The Griffin Report*, a publication featuring news of the retail food industry of the Northeast. The message communicates the enduring quest of the company: to produce the highest quality all-natural flour.

Pancakes from Scratch.
Scratch the Chemicals!

King Arthur Flour is naturally white and pure — never bleached, never bromated — and higher in gluten than ordinary flours.

We mill King Arthur Flour from the best wheat money can buy. What's more, we use only the choicest part of the wheat berry, the heart. So our flour has more natural protein, or gluten, than ordinary flours.

Everything you make, from the bread you bake to the pancakes for your breakfast, will have a pure wholesome aroma, be more nutritious and taste better. Naturally. Compared to King Arthur, other flours are strictly run of the mill.

KING ARTHUR FLOUR

Do you love to bake? Write or call for our baker's catalogue, full of tools, ingredients, information and recipes at King Arthur Flour Baker's Catalogue, P.O. Box 876, Department PM, Norwich, Vermont 05055 or call 1-800-777-4434.

Surfing the Net? Visit our home page at http://www.kingarthurflour.com

The message that no chemicals are ever added to King Arthur Flour remained an important part of the company's advertising from the early days up to recent times, as seen in this 1996 magazine ad.

The theme of this mid-1990s advertising campaign is that the entire family can be involved in baking.

A photography crew is involved in a 1990s advertising campaign shoot. Brinna and Frank Sands are pictured second and fourth from the left.

For Everyone Who Puts Their Best Into Their Baking.

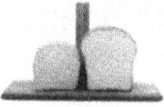

Breads rise higher with our flour because it has so much more gluten.

Since gluten absorbs moisture, King Arthur Flour keeps your baked goods fresher, longer.

The premium wheats in our flour assure you consistently great results.

Our Baker's Catalogue is a shopper's paradise of baking ideas, ingredients and accessories.

Your baked goods will have better aroma and flavor because we never add any chemicals.

King Arthur Flour is perfect for all your favorite recipes.

Our flour is so protein-rich, you can get an extra loaf of bread in every 5 lb bag.

Write and tell us about your experiences baking with King Arthur Flour. We'd love to hear from you.

What is it that all of the best bakers put into their baking? Well, there's their time, their effort, and, of course, their King Arthur Flour. Because for over two hundred years, only King Arthur has been putting nothing but the best into their flour. No bleaches. No bromates. And never any added chemicals. Just the protein-rich hearts of the finest winter and spring wheats in the land. Use King Arthur Flour. It's perfect for anyone who puts only their best into their baking.

If you want a free copy of our great baker's catalogue, write to us at King Arthur Flour, P.O. Box 876, Dept. V, Norwich, VT 05055 or call 1-800-777-4434

As distribution of King Arthur Flour increased with new stores added across the country in the 1990s, the locations were often touted in the advertising. In February 2003, King Arthur Flour, for the first time, was sold in stores in 50 states.

In 1992, the King Arthur Flour Company started the Life Skills Bread Share program to introduce the joy of baking to middle school students. Baking instructor Michael Jubinsky (middle) teaches in Middletown, Connecticut, in April 1994. More than 40,000 students have participated in the program since its inception.

Instructor Robin Rice teaches a Life Skills Bread Share class.

On November 12–14, 1993, Brinna Sands discussed bread baking at the New England Culinary Institute weekend.

Baking education has always been an important focus of the King Arthur Flour Company. This emphasis increased even more at the end of the 20th century with King Arthur's national baking classes. Visiting cities across the United States, the King Arthur Flour Company's free baking classes show audiences how to make artisan breads and sweet dough recipes. They have been attended by thousands and remain a popular company program, with requests coming in almost daily to have one the classes visit different parts of the country. In Norwich, Vermont, the King Arthur Flour Company teaches baking year-round at the Baking Education Center.

BAKER'S MECCA

Both a catalog and a retail store, King Arthur Flour Company keeps baking lovers coming back for more

By Claire Hopley

KING ARTHUR FLOUR
SANDS, TAYLOR & WOOD CO.

When you make it big in retail, you put out a catalog. Right?

That is the way it often happens. But the King Arthur Flour Company bucked the trend and did it the other way around. Its catalog of baking ingredients and utensils appeared in 1990. With premium flours, specialty sugars, and hard-to-find grains, it wooed home bakers.

Soon fans came knocking on the warehouse door. "They didn't want to pay shipping charges," laughs Joe Caron, public relations director, "so they'd just back the family station wagon right up to our loading dock."

The company got the message, and in 1992, it converted the warehouse into King Arthur Flour Baker's Store. Now, there's a cookbook nook where trucks used to load flour, and a kitchen where store manager Cindy Fountain bakes fragrant treats, such as Ginger Chocolate Chip Scones and Irish Currant Bread. And, an surprise, these are eager customers, snapping up products and just generally enjoying every minute in their baking mecca.

Located outside Norwich in Vermont—the state with the smallest population of any in the country—King Arthur Flour Baker's Store does not exactly sit in a high-traffic spot. Nonetheless, gross sales of $275,000 in the first year of business, 1992, zoomed to $3.1 million in 1998.

LIFESTYLE

Beverly Mills & Alicia Ross

Easy meal for before the holiday

Rising to the occasion

A class gives tips and shortcuts on baking breads and other treats. It offers something for novices as well as veterans in the kitchen.

The *Topeka Capital-Journal* and the *Dayton Daily News* featured articles on the art of wholesome homemade bread baking.

Four

RECIPES AND COOKBOOKS

Recipes using King Arthur Flour have always been available through the company. Some of these reached customers as inserts in flour bags. Today, ideal recipes for baking with King Arthur Flour are printed on each bag. Yet, whether at the beginning of the 20th or 21st centuries, one strategy was always important to the company: helping customers have great success with King Arthur Flour.

It is interesting to see on the following pages how the recipes offered by the company were a reflection of the United States at that specific time. For example, during World War II, when eggs and milk were of limited supply, the cake-pan-cake recipe came out. It is simple to make, mixes right in the pan, and does not call for eggs or milk. As a quality recipe, its popularity continued even after the war.

The *King Arthur Flour 200th Anniversary Cookbook* came out in 1990. For many, this was the most important book on baking ever published. More than 100,000 copies of the cookbook have been sold. In 2003, the *Baker's Companion* cookbook came out, and it was an immediate success, selling more than 75,000 copies in less than one year. It received the James Beard Award for cookbook of the year and received amazing reviews from top bakers and chefs. In 2004, the *Cookie Companion* cookbook, featuring more than 500 cookie recipes, hit bookstores across the country and continued the King Arthur trend of strong praise from reviewers.

Since King Arthur Flour has been milled to consistently high specifications going back to its inception in 1896, the recipes offered by the company through the years are still relevant today.

The King Arthur Flour Company and the Wheat Flour Institute in Chicago, Illinois, teamed up to offer a small book of yeast-bread recipes in the early 1900s. Copy in the book read, "Transforming fine white flour into satiny smooth dough, and watching it transform itself into puffy light rolls and bread is one of the major satisfactions in cooking." This recipe for sour cream rolls was featured in the book.

I C E   B O X   R O L L S

This recipe makes a dough that will keep indefinitely in your
ice box.   Use only a small amount to make hot rolls whenever
you want them.

TO MAKE DOUGH: Prepare separately, (1) Scald 1 quart milk
and while warm add 1 cup butter. (2) Dissolve 2 cakes compressed yeast in ½ cup warm water.   (3) 1 cup mashed potatoes.
(4) Mix together 7 cups KING ARTHUR FLOUR, 1 teaspoon soda, 2
teaspoons baking powder, 1½ teaspoons salt, and 1 cup sugar.
When milk is cool mix all ingredients together, beat thoroughly, and let stand in warm room for 2 hours.   Then add 6 cups
KING ARTHUR FLOUR, knead thoroughly, cover and place in ice
box for 24 hours before using.

TO BAKE: Pinch off desired amount dough, roll out, cut with
biscuit cutter, slice partially through middle of each, and
fold over double, pinching ends together and adding melted
butter between folds.   Keep in warm room until light and
bake in quick oven.   Always keep unused dough covered in the
ice box.

SANDS, TAYLOR & WOOD COMPANY

28 Fitchburg Street
Somerville, Massachusetts

This early recipe for rolls offers convenience; it "makes a dough that will keep indefinitely in
your ice box. Use only a small amount to make hot rolls whenever you want them." It was typed
up when the offices were in Somerville, Massachusetts.

SWEDISH COFFEE BREAD

YIELD: 2 LOAVES

1 cup milk
6 tablespoon margarine or butter
2 eggs
½ cup sugar
1½ teaspoon salt
2 pkg. active dry yeast
1 teaspoon crushed cardamon or
6 whole cardamon seeds (crushed)
4½ to 5 cups King Arthur Flour

Combine milk and shortening in saucepan and heat until lukewarm. Pour into mixing bowl, add eggs, sugar, salt, yeast, crushed cardamon and 1 cup King Arthur Flour and beat for 2 minutes with electric beater. Gradually add balance of flour stirring by hand until the dough no longer sticks to the sides of the bowl.

Now follow directions on inside of folder, place dough on floured board, knead for 8 to 10 minutes, let rise in greased bowl until double in bulk, punch down, and divide in half. Now cut each half into 3 pieces, roll each piece into a rope and braid. (If you wish, you may form the loaves without braiding) Place loaves in 2 greased bread pans, brush tops of loaves with melted shortening and sprinkle with a mixture of cinnamon and sugar, let rise until double in bulk, and bake in a preheated 350 degree oven for about 30 minutes.

EGG BREAD "CHALE"

YIELD: 3 LOAVES

2 cups water
6 tablespoon shortening
2 tablespoon sugar
1 tablespoon salt
3 eggs (reserve 1 egg yolk)
2 pkg. active dry yeast
6½ to 7 cups King Arthur Flour

Combine water and shortening in saucepan and heat until lukewarm. Pour into mixing bowl, add sugar, salt, eggs, yeast and 2 cups King Arthur Flour and beat for 2 minutes with electric beater. Gradually add balance of flour, stirring by hand until the dough pulls away from the sides of the bowl.

Now follow directions on inside of folder, place dough on floured board, knead for 6 to 7 minutes, let rise in greased bowl until double in bulk, punch down and divide into 3 parts. Divide each part into 3 more parts and roll each into a rope. Now braid the 3 ropes into a loaf. (If you wish, you may form the 3 loaves without braiding)

Place loaves in 3 greased bread pans, brush top of loaves with mixture of reserved egg yolk, 1 tablespoon water and dash of salt, let rise until double in bulk, and bake in preheated 400 degree oven for 35 to 45 minutes.

KING ARTHUR FLOUR

"BREAD BAKING MADE EASY"

NEVER   BLEACHED

Remember the aroma in Grandmother's kitchen when she made her own bread. It brings back some wonderful memories, doesn't it?

But Grandmother's bread-baking was a major task, requiring almost 10 hours from start to finish. Now, however, by using this new easy method, only 4 hours are needed. Start your bread after breakfast, eat it for lunch.

And you can use the same flour Grandmother used, NEVER BLEACHED KING ARTHUR FLOUR, higher in protein for better bread, yet unexcelled for cakes and pastries, milled only from hard spring wheat, and white as nature intended it to be, without any bleaching.

In a day when food additives are so much the subject of doubts and misgivings, isn't it reassuring to know that KING ARTHUR FLOUR is still pure and unbleached? For your health's sake, use it always.

This pamphlet for King Arthur Flour focused on easy bread baking. The opening copy encouraged readers to "start your bread after breakfast, eat it for lunch." Two of the recipes, Swedish Coffee Bread and Egg Bread "Chale," are included on the left.

CAKE-PAN CAKE
(a delicious, moist, dark chocolate cake)

1½ cups King Arthur Flour
1 cup sugar
3 tablespoons cocoa
1 teaspoon soda
½ teaspoon salt

6 tablespoons cooking oil (or melted shortening)
1 tablespoon vinegar
1 teaspoon vanilla
1 cup cold water

Put dry ingredients into sifter. Sift directly into ungreased cake pan (8" square). Make 3 holes in dry mixture. Pour cooking oil in first hole. Pour vinegar in second hole. Pour vanilla in third hole. Pour cold water over all. Stir with fork until evenly blended. Bake 35-40 minutes in 350° oven. Invert to cool and remove from pan; or frost right in the pan.

for Stay-Fresh Cake, USE KING ARTHUR UNBLEACHED FLOUR

During World War II, eggs, milk, and shortening were in short supply. The King Arthur Flour Company came out with cake-pan-cake recipes in response. Note how the recipe uses no eggs or milk and can be mixed right in the pan. Its simplicity and quality made this a popular recipe from the 1940s into the 1950s.

84

EASY HOME BAKING

Easy Home Baking, a collection of recipes for breads, rolls, cakes, cookies, pastries, and desserts, was offered by the company during the late 1950s. The introduction reads, "This book is for every housewife to make her baking easy. For those who have never had the fun of baking or who have never tried, we hope this book will show you how easy, economical, and satisfying you can make so many good things to eat for you and your family." Some of these recipes have been printed on the following pages.

TESTED RECIPES FOR BREADS, ROLLS, CAKES, COOKIES, PASTRIES AND DESSERTS

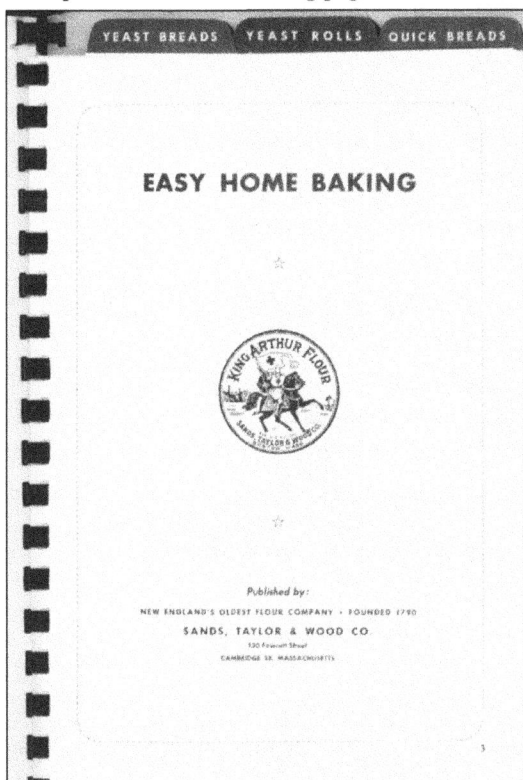

YEAST BREADS   YEAST ROLLS   QUICK BREADS

EASY HOME BAKING

Published by:
NEW ENGLAND'S OLDEST FLOUR COMPANY · FOUNDED 1790

SANDS, TAYLOR & WOOD CO.
130 Franklin Street
CAMBRIDGE 39, MASSACHUSETTS

WHITE BREAD

(STRAIGHT DAY-TIME METHOD)

Baking Time: 50 Minutes   *Oven Temp.: 400°*

RECIPE

Ingredients	6 Loaves	4 Loaves	2 Loaves
King Arthur Flour	17¾ cups	11¾ cups	6 cups
Milk	3 cups	2 cups	1 cup
Water	3¼ cups	2¼ cups	1¼ cups
Yeast	2 cakes	1 to 2 cakes	1 cake
(Compressed			
or granular)			
Sugar	6 tablespoons	¼ cup	2 tablespoons
Salt	2 tablespoons	4 teaspoons	2 teaspoons
Shortening	3 tablespoons	2 tablespoons	1 tablespoon

PROCEDURE

MIXING

1. Crumble the yeast into ¼ cup of lukewarm water—and let it soften for 5 minutes.

2. Scald the milk. To scald milk, bring it slowly to a high temperature, but keep it below the boiling point. When milk is heated directly over the fire, you must watch it and stir it to prevent scorching. Milk boils at a lower temperature than water. After scalding, add sugar, salt and cold water. Stir thoroughly until salt and sugar are dissolved. Pour into a large mixing bowl. Allow milk to cool until lukewarm.

3. Pour softened yeast into the lukewarm milk mixture. Stir until well mixed—no chunks of yeast should remain separate after stirring.

4. Add half of the sifted flour to the milk mixture. Stir the dough until flour and liquids are thoroughly mixed into a batter. Note: Adding half of the flour at this time prevents streaks in the bread and helps to make a moist loaf which will keep fresh longer.

5. Melt the shortening. Allow to cool and add to the batter and stir thoroughly.

6. Finally add the remaining sifted flour and mix well. Stir flour into batter until batter takes up the flour.

13

The opening recipe from *Easy Home Baking* was a simple daytime method for making white bread.

RAISIN BREAD

Add ¼ cup of raisins to any bread dough after the first kneading.

Proceed with bread making according to directions.

NUT BREAD

Use the recipe for white bread. Add 1 additional tablespoon of sugar and ¼ cup of chopped nuts for each loaf of nut bread to be made. Add the nuts to the dough at the end of the first kneading.

WHOLE WHEAT BREAD

Time: 50 Minutes. Temp.: 425° for 10 minutes, 375° remaining time.

4 loaves	Ingredients	1 loaf
6 cups	King Arthur Flour	1½ cups
6 cups	100% Whole Wheat Flour	1½ cups
2 cups	Milk	½ cup
2¼ cups	Water	⅔ cup
½ cup	Sirup or Brown Sugar	2 tbsps.
2 cakes	Yeast	1 cake
2½ tbsps.	Salt	2 tsps.
⅓ cup	Shortening	2 tbsps.

1. Crumble yeast in ¼ cup lukewarm water. Let it stand 10 minutes. Scald milk, add salt and sirup, let cool.

2. Combine the milk and water mixtures, add the whole wheat flour and beat well.

3. Add the melted shortening. When mixed in, add the white flour gradually to make a dough stiff enough to handle when placed on board.

4. Lightly flour a bread board, turn the dough out on it and knead well. Place dough in greased bowl, oil the top, and cover. Set it in a warm place away from drafts. Let rise until double in bulk.

5. Punch down. Let rise again. Divide dough into equal portions and shape into loaves. Place into oiled bread pans. Let rise until double in bulk. Bake.

SALT RISING BREAD

Quantity: 1 loaf. Time: 50 Minutes. Temp.: 400°.

  3 cups King Arthur Flour
  1 cup milk
  2 tablespoons white corn meal
  1 teaspoon salt
  1 tablespoon sugar
  1 tablespoon shortening

1. Scald the milk, and cool to lukewarm. Add sugar, shortening, salt and corn meal.

2. Place in a fruit jar or heavy crock and set in water 120°. Let stand for 6 or 7 hours until fermentation can be noted.

3. Add 1½ cups of flour to make a sponge. Beat vigorously. Set sponge away in water at 120° until very light.

4. Add remaining flour to make a dough stiff enough to knead.

5. Knead for 10 minutes, place immediately into oiled baking pan. Allow to rise at least twice its original bulk. Bake. This bread is never as light as a yeast bread.

OATMEAL BREAD

Quantity: 3 loaves. Time: 50 Minutes. Temp.: 425° for 10 minutes, 375° for remaining time.

  7 cups King Arthur Flour
{ 1½ cups oatmeal
  3 cups water
  ½ teaspoon salt
  2 cakes yeast
  ¾ cup lukewarm water
  2 teaspoons salt
  3 tablespoons melted shortening
  3 tablespoons brown sugar

1. Steam oatmeal in the salted water until cooked. Cool.

2. Crumble yeast in ¼ cup lukewarm water and let stand 10 minutes.

3. To the lukewarm oatmeal add the dissolved yeast, salt, sugar, and melted shortening.

4. Add flour to make a stiff dough. Then turn out on a floured board and knead until elastic.

5. Place in an oiled bowl, cover, set in a warm place, and let rise until double in bulk.

6. Punch dough down, let rise again.

7. Shape into loaves, cover and let rise until double in bulk, then bake.

19

Variations using the white bread recipe were next in *Easy Home Baking,* including raisin bread and nut bread. Other breads followed, such as whole-wheat bread, salt rising bread, and oatmeal bread.

SHORTCAKE BISCUITS

2 cups KING ARTHUR FLOUR
1 tablespoon sugar
1/2 teaspoon salt
4 teaspoon baking powder
1/3 cup shortening
2/3 cup milk

Put first 4 ingredients in a mixing bowl and stir. Cut in the shortening with the side of a fork until it resembles coarse crumbs. Next add the milk, lightly stirring and tossing with a fork until all the flour has been absorbed. Do not mix more than necessary because you do not want to strengthen the gluten in the flour.

Sprinkle 1 tablespoon of flour on your board and gently roll the dough in it. Then press the dough out with your fingertips until it is about 1 inch thick. Cut dough into 10 pieces. Gently round the corners of each piece of dough with your fingers and bake on an ungreased cookie sheet in a preheated 425 degree oven for about 15 minutes.

Biscuits are best when served warm.

ORANGE FLUFF CAKE

6 egg whites
1/2 teaspoon salt
3/4 cup sugar
— — — — — —
6 egg yolks
3/4 cup sugar
1-1/2 teaspoon lemon extract
1/2 cup orange juice (frozen or fresh)
1-1/2 cups KING ARTHUR FLOUR
1 teaspoon baking powder

In a large bowl, beat egg whites with salt to form moist, glossy peaks. Gradually beat in sugar. Set aside. In another bowl beat egg yolks and sugar until thick. Blend in extract and juice; beat in flour mixed with baking powder. Pour egg yolk mixture into egg white mixture. FOLD IN. DO NOT BEAT.

Bake in a 10 inch ungreased angel food cake pan for 1 hour at 325 degrees. Invert to cool before removing from pan. Ice with your favorite frosting.

Unsweetened pineapple juice may be substituted for orange juice.

＊ ＊ ＊ ＊ ＊

What is a cake recipe doing in a booklet entitled *"More Bread Recipes"*? Well, after you have tried everything else, make this cake for yourself. You deserve it.

For simple variations in your white bread, try adding a cup of raisins or 2 tablespoons of caroway seed to the dough, just after using your electric beater.

Tests have shown that bread stales faster when stored in a refrigerator than it does in a bread box at room temperature.

More Bread Recipes, As Easy, As Ever was put together when the company was in Andover, Massachusetts (1978–1983). These two recipes are for shortcake biscuits and orange fluff cake.

A Short Course

with

KING ARTHUR FLOUR®

in

Baking with Yeast

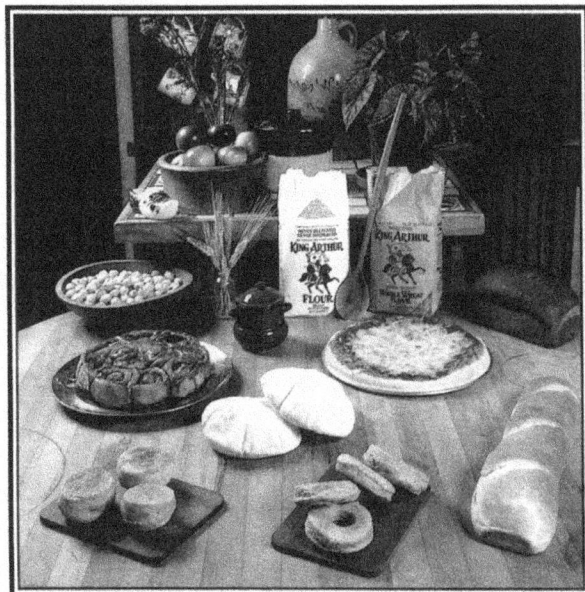

A Short Course with King Arthur Flour in Baking with Yeast came out in 1985 and was revised in 1989.

A Few Preliminaries...

Why would you want to bake a loaf of bread, especially when there are so many varieties available at the store?

Well...making a loaf of bread, turning all that sticky lumpy mess into a loaf of <u>real</u> bread, feels different from buying a loaf that someone else, or some mystery machine has made. If you haven't made bread yet, we won't tell you what that feeling is, or try to describe it.

But...when you are holding a slice of warm bread in your hand, one that you made yourself, you'll feel that feeling, plus, from that slice of bread, you will get more energy than you can from any other kind of food! It can help you lose weight. It can be packed with things that are good for you (and things that are not so good when you're in the mood for something sinful!). By cooking it differently, you can transform a basic bread dough into pizza, pita bread, bagels, English muffins, sticky buns... You can do things with it that no one has thought of yet because that's part of the magic of making bread. It can be anything you want today, or something that pops into your head tomorrow!

So... let's start with the basic bread "formula." If you make a commitment to learn that combination of ingredients, and make it so familiar that your hands know what to do without your head having to think about it, you'll discover how easy and quick it is to bake with yeast "from scratch." You'll be able to put in those "extras" that commercial enterprises do not.

And...most important, you will discover that baking with yeast is fun! It is somewhere between making mudpies and sculpting, a mixture of the earthy and the sublime. And most likely, your experiments with yeast, unlike those of your earlier experiments with mud, will be received with great anticipation and enthusiasm!

Brinna Sands, 1985
Revised 1989

On the Cover: A collection of some of the things that can be made with the Basic Dough. Clockwise from upper left: Sticky Buns (page 22), Pita Bread (page 21), Pizza (page 20), Hearth Bread (page 4), Bagels (page 17), and English Muffins (page 16).

3

Brinna Sands's introduction to *A Short Course with King Arthur Flour in Baking with Yeast* was followed by recipes from it: King Arthur's basic white bread, whole-wheat bread, oatmeal bread, anadama bread, and rye bread.

This recipe for basic white bread mentions in small print at the end, "The best pans to use for bread baking are darkened aluminum or other dark metal. Glass pans are also fine, although your cruse is apt to be thicker and you may find that you want to reduce your oven temperature by 25 degrees."

Clockwise from upper left: Sticky Buns cut partially through and formed into a ring (page 22), Doughnuts (page 34), "Arthur's" Festival bread (page 31), A "Mock Braid"enclosing Sticky Buns filling, 2 slices of Sticky Bun Bread, Whole Wheat Bread with added Raisins (page 26), and in the center, Portugese Sweet Bread (page 32).

KING ARTHUR'S BASIC WHITE BREAD

This recipe is a classic white bread designed for active, dry yeast (not the new rapid rise yeast) with a traditional rising and baking process, to be baked in 4 1/2 x 8 1/2 inch bread pans. (You will find directions for rapid rise yeast, if you wish to use it, on the packet.) You can also use larger bread pans if that is what you have. Your bread will simply be "shorter and fatter!"

2 cups water
2 tablespoon sugar or honey
1 tablespoon or packet active dry yeast
1 tablespoon salt (or less if desired)
2 tablespoons vegetable oil, butter or a combination of both
1/2 cup dry milk (optional)
6 cups King Arthur unbleached flour

Blend Ingredients

To 2 cups hot water, add and let dissolve in 3 successive stages, the sugar or honey, yeast and salt. When all three are dissolved, add the dry milk, softened butter and 5 1/2 cups of King Arthur flour measured according to the directions on the bag. Pour the other 1/2 cup of flour on the board where you intend to knead.

Knead and Rise

With a large spoon, stir the flour into the liquid brew until it begins to hold together. Turn it out onto the floured board and knead until the dough begins to feel as if it really belongs together, adding only enough more flour to keep it from sticking to the board, or you. Let it rest while you clean and grease your bowl. Continue kneading the relaxed dough until it feels smooth and springy. Form it into a nice ball, place it in the greased bowl turning it so the top is greased, cover it, and place it where it will be warm and cozy (no drafts!). Let this rise until it is doubled.

Shape

When you can poke your finger in the dough without it bouncing back at you, knock it down, turn it out onto your floured board and knead out any stray bubbles. Cut in half, form 2 loaves and place them in your greased bread pans.*

Bake

Let your loaves rise until almost doubled (about 45 minutes), place in a pre-heated 350°F oven and bake 35 minutes. Another baking method is to let the loaves rise for only 20 to 30 minutes, place them in a cold oven, set the temperature at 400°F for 15 minutes and lower it to 350°F for a further 20 to 25 minutes. A longer baking period produces a crustier bread with a slightly dryer interior.

*Here is a hint about greasing bread or cake pans. Perhaps when you were growing up, you were taught to flour your pans after you greased them. If you grease your pans with butter, flouring them serves to absorb the moisture in the butter which is always present even when you can't see it. Shortening, on the other hand, contains no moisture, so flouring is not necessary, one of the few situations in baking where even good King Arthur can't help! Just make sure King Arthur is in the dough you put in the pan. That is where its natural strength and chemical free aroma will do its best for you! The best pans to use for bread are darkened aluminum or other dark metal. Glass pans are also fine, although your crust is apt to be thicker and you may find that you want to reduce your oven temperature by 25°F.

KING ARTHUR'S STONE-GROUND
WHOLE WHEAT BREAD

Bread made with stone-ground whole wheat flour is robust, hearty and especially nutritious because it contains the vitamin and iron-rich germ of the wheat and also the fiber rich bran layer. It makes wonderful sandwiches, and is a great accompaniment to meats, cheese or hot steaming soups.

Whole wheat bread will not rise as high as white bread. As gluten strands are developing through kneading, the tiny pieces of bran tend to shred them a bit causing some of the carbon dioxide bubbles created by the yeast to escape, creating the denser texture associated with whole grain breads. To soften the bran and thus to minimize this shredding, we use the sponge method for this recipe. We are going to use a combination of whole wheat and unbleached white flours here which will give you the benefits of both. If you want to use whole wheat completely, do so.

2 cups water
1/2 cup dry milk (optional)
1/2 cup brown sugar, honey or molasses (less if desired)
1 tablespoon salt (less if desired)
1 tablespoon or packet active dry yeast
1/2 stick butter or 1/4 cup vegetable oil
3 cups King Arthur stone-ground whole wheat flour
3 to 4 cups King Arthur unbleached flour

To 2 cups of hot water, add and let dissolve in 3 successive stages, 1 tablespoon of your sweetener, the yeast and the salt. When all three are dissolved, add the balance of the sweetener, the vegetable oil or softened butter and the 3 cups of King Arthur stone-ground whole wheat flour. Mix this together with a large spoon and let it sit for at least 2 hours, or all day if that's more convenient. This sponge will bubble away, softening the bran, and developing flavor while you go about something else.

About 1 1/2 to 2 hours before you want to serve your bread, add most of the remaining flour, 3 cups if you have used brown sugar, 3 1/2 cups if you have used honey or molasses. Sprinkle the rest on your kneading board. You will have to use a little elbow grease to incorporate the flour into the sponge, but work it in as thoroughly as you can before you turn it out onto the floured board. Knead the dough until it is springy and no longer sticky, adding only enough more flour to keep it from sticking to you or the board. Cut the dough in half and form two loaves. Place in greased bread pans and let rise until almost doubled. See King Arthur's Basic White Bread to "Bake" (page 25).

Recipes like this one calling for King Arthur whole-wheat flour continue to be popular today.

Variations

Try adding 3 tablespoons of cinnamon and 1 cup of raisins to your initial sponge. Or after you've added and kneaded in the balance of your flour, roll half your dough (enough for 1 loaf) into an 8 by 14 inch rectangle. Spread with a thin layer of honey or brown sugar leaving an inch around the outside edge. Sprinkle heavily with cinnamon and raisins. Roll up from the short edge, pinch the seam and ends together thoroughly (don't worry about how it looks), and place seam side down in your greased pan. Let rise and bake according to whatever method you choose.

KING ARTHUR'S OATMEAL BREAD

Oatmeal bread is almost as popular in New England as bread made completely with wheat. Oatmeal breads originated in cool, damp, northern areas where oats grow more successfully than wheat. Oats have long been a staple of the Scots who have developed many uses for it.

While the oats we are most familiar with have been rolled, it is also possible to buy steel cut oats at health food and specialty stores. Steel cut oats have been cut and steamed as have rolled oats, but they have not been through the rolling process so they look more like cracked wheat. They add a crunchy texture to bread.

2 cups boiling water
1 cup rolled or steel cut oats
1/2 cup dry milk (optional)
1/2 cup honey (or molasses)
1 tablespoon or packet of active dry yeast
1 tablespoon (or less) salt
1/2 stick butter or 1/4 cup vegetable oil
5 cups King Arthur unbleached flour

Pour the water into a mixing bowl and add the oats and honey. Stir thoroughly and let cool to room temperature. Add the yeast, allowing it to dissolve before adding the dry milk, the salt and the softened butter. Stir in 4 1/2 cups of King Arthur flour and pour the remaining 1/2 cup on the board where you intend to knead. Mix the flour into the dough until it begins to hold together and pull away from the sides of the bowl. Turn it out onto the floured board and knead until it begins to feel springy. Let the dough rest while you clean and grease your bowl. Continue kneading, adding only enough flour to keep the dough from getting sticky. When it is smooth and springy, form it into a ball and place it in the greased bowl, turning it to grease the top. From this point continue from "Shape" under King Arthur's Basic White Bread (page 25).

Classics•27

This recipe for King Arthur's oatmeal bread features one cup of either rolled or steel cut oats. Steps used in the recipe for basic white bread (on pages 91 and 92) are adopted for the end of this oatmeal bread recipe.

KING ARTHUR'S ANADAMA BREAD

As the Scots replaced some of the wheat in their breads with their local oats, our forebears here in New England responded in kind with "Indian meal,"or cornmeal. The name Anadama, as the story goes, was originally an oath bestowed upon Anna by her hungry fisherman husband. It seem that she had abandoned him to a meal of cornmeal mush and molasses. He, in a burst of frustration and creativity, added flour, salt, butter and yeast and produced this now familiar and traditional New England bread.

> 2 cups boiling water
> 1/2 cup cornmeal
> 1 cup dry milk (optional)
> 1/2 cup dark unsulphured molasses
> 1 tablespoon or packet active dry yeast
> 1 tablespoon (or less) salt
> 1/2 stick butter or 1/4 cup vegetable oil
> 5 cups King Arthur unbleached flour

As you add the cornmeal to the hot water, and as it cools, it's important to stir thoroughly, so that it doesn't lump. Proceed with this recipe as you would for King Arthur's Oatmeal Bread (page 27).

KING ARTHUR FLOUR®

NEVER BLEACHED
NEVER BROMATED

KING ARTHUR
FLOUR
ALL-PURPOSE
NATURALLY PURE
& WHOLESOME

KING ARTHUR
STONE GROUND
WHOLE WHEAT
FLOUR
100% OF THE
WHEAT GERM
& BRAN

Dedicated to the
Pure Joy of Baking.℠

From *A Short Course with King Arthur Flour in Baking with Yeast*, this recipe for anadama bread uses five cups of King Arthur all-purpose flour. Steps used in the recipe for oatmeal bread (page 93) are followed at the end.

Yeast Breads

SNUGGLE BUNS

½ cup warm water
½ cake fresh yeast, or 2 packages
   (2 scant tablespoons) dry yeast
⅔ cup honey
⅓ cup softened butter

3 cups milk, warmed to about 100°F.
2 teaspoons salt
2 eggs, beaten
about 10 cups King Arthur flour

Pour water into large mixing bowl and sprinkle on yeast. When yeast has softened, stir in honey, butter, milk, and salt, and mix until well blended. Stir in eggs. Gradually add flour, mixing well, until dough is soft but not too sticky. Form into a ball and place in a lightly greased bowl. Cover and let rise until doubled. Punch down and let rise again. Meanwhile, make filling.

FILLING:

4 ounces chopped dates
1 cup water
1 teaspoon vanilla extract
grated rind of 1 lemon

1 large apple, peeled and chopped fine
⅓ cup finely chopped nuts
extra butter, cold

Place dates and water in a saucepan and cook until thickened. Stir in vanilla and let cool. When dough is ready to use, add grated lemon rind, chopped apple, and chopped nuts to date mixture.

Punch down dough after second rising. On a floured surface, pinch off small pieces (about ¼ cup each) of dough and shape into flattened rounds. Place about 1 tablespoon filling in the center of each round, dot with cold butter, and bring dough together, pressing edges to close. Place smooth side down in baking pan. Let rise until nearly doubled. Bake in a preheated 375°F. oven for about 30 minutes, or until golden. Remove from oven and cool thoroughly before glazing. Makes about 4 dozen.

GLAZE:

1 cup powdered sugar
½ teaspoon vanilla extract
½ teaspoon lemon extract
dash salt

2 tablespoons water or milk (enough to
   attain proper consistency)
½ cup chopped nuts (optional)

Stir together sugar, extracts, salt, and water and mix until smooth. Drizzle over rolls. Sprinkle with chopped nuts if desired. Rolls freeze well before glazing.

In 1987, *Yankee* magazine published their *First Annual Great New England Cook-off Cookbook*. First prize in the yeast breads category went to this Snuggle Buns recipe, made with 10 cups of King Arthur Flour.

In the *Second Annual Great New England Coof-off Cookbook* in 1988, the first prize in the yeast breads category was the recipe for tomato bread. It calls for six to six and a half cups of King Arthur unbleached flour.

Salads

Cut off and discard top and bottom from the bell peppers; remove and discard seeds and membranes. Wash peppers and drain well. In a small bowl beat the cream cheese until fluffy, using an electric mixer on high speed. Add the Worcestershire sauce, lemon juice, mayonnaise, onion, seasoned salt, and garlic and beat again at medium speed until all ingredients are well blended. Fill each pepper with the cheese mixture and wrap tightly in plastic wrap. Chill the filled peppers for at least 2 hours.

To serve, line 4 salad plates with lettuce leaves. Cut each tomato into 4 slices and place 2 slices on each plate. Using a hot knife, cut each pepper crosswise into 4 rounds. Place one green pepper round and one yellow pepper round atop the tomato slices. Sprinkle the crabmeat over the pepper slices and top with the cocktail sauce. Serves 4.

Lynda Sarkisian
Inman, South Carolina

Yeast Breads

TOMATO BREAD

2 cups tomato juice	1 teaspoon salt
½ cup tomato sauce	½ teaspoon dried sweet basil
2 tablespoons butter or olive oil	¾ teaspoon dried oregano
6 to 6½ cups King Arthur unbleached flour	¼ teaspoon ground rosemary
2 packages (2 scant tablespoons) dry yeast	¼ teaspoon ground fennel
3 tablespoons sugar	1 small garlic clove, crushed

Heat tomato juice, sauce, and butter or oil to 120°F. In large bowl combine 3 cups of the flour with the yeast, sugar, salt, basil, oregano, rosemary, and fennel; add warmed tomato mixture and garlic. Mix with dough hook (or by hand) for 3 minutes or 300 strokes, scraping sides of bowl frequently. Add 3 to 3½ cups additional flour and turn out onto floured board to knead when dough is firm enough to be handled. Add enough flour so dough is not sticky, and knead well. Place dough in a greased bowl, cover, and let rise in a warm place until doubled, about an hour. Punch down, let rest for 15 minutes, and shape into two large loaves. Place in greased bread pans, cover loosely, and let rise until nearly doubled, about 45 minutes. Bake at 375°F for 10 minutes, then reduce heat to 350°F and bake for another 30 minutes, or until loaves sound hollow when tapped. Remove from pans and cool on rack. Tastes great sliced and toasted in the oven topped with pepperoni, green olives, and cheese. Makes 2 loaves.

Michelle Rich
Argos, Indiana

From 1990 to 1993, King Arthur held WinterBake, a national baking competition with more than 1,000 annual entries. The 1993 judges are, from left to right, Elizabeth Alston, *Woman's Day* food editor; Albert Kumin, White House pastry chef; Julia Child, chef, author, and television personality; Bernard Clayton Jr., bread baking author; Marion Cunningham, "modern day Fannie Farmer;" and Jim Dodge, pastry chef and author. Brinna and Frank Sands II are pictured on the stairs.

The junior grand prize at the 1991 WinterBake was awarded for this recipe for Chunk Wild Cookies.

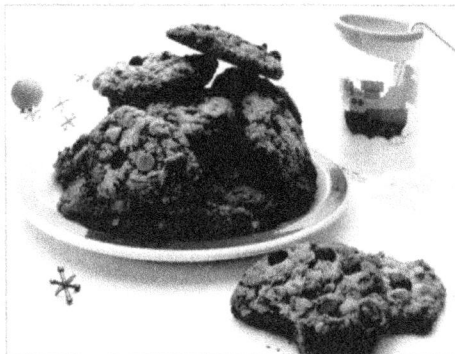

Chunk Wild Cookies

1 cup butter
1 cup white sugar
1 cup light brown sugar
2 eggs
1 teaspoon vanilla extract
2 1/2 cups oatmeal
2 cups King Arthur Unbleached Flour
1 teaspoon baking powder
1 teaspoon baking soda
6 ounces peanut butter chips
6 ounces chocolate chips
4 ounces grated white chocolate
1 1/2 cups chopped walnuts

Preheat oven to 375°F. Cream together butter and sugars. Add eggs and vanilla. Using a blender or food processor, grind the oatmeal until it turns to powder. In a separate bowl, mix the oatmeal, flour, baking powder, and baking soda. Add peanut butter chips, chocolate chips, white chocolate, and chopped walnuts. Drop by tablespoonfuls, 2 inches apart, onto an ungreased baking sheet. Bake for approximately 7 minutes.

Sarah Nist, Montpelier, VT

MUFFINS & QUICK BREADS

Savory Sausage Muffins

16 oz. ground sausage, cooked & drained
1 small onion, chopped
2 eggs
1 1/4 cups sour cream
3 tablespoons Dijon mustard
1/4 cup oil or melted margarine
1 teaspoon paprika
1/2 teaspoon black pepper
1 cup cornmeal
1/2 cup King Arthur Unbleached Flour
1/2 cup King Arthur Whole Wheat Flour
1 tablespoon baking powder
1 teaspoon salt
1/4 cup Parmesan cheese
4 oz. grated Cheddar cheese

Cook sausage until almost done. Add chopped onion and cook until transparent. Drain off excess fat and allow to cool while preparing other ingredients.

In large bowl, beat eggs; add sour cream, mustard, oil, paprika and pepper. In a medium bowl combine cornmeal, flours, baking powder and salt. Slowly add to sour cream and egg mixture. Combine cheeses with mixture; lastly add the cooled sausage and onions. Place in muffin cups that have been sprayed with a non-stick vegetable spray.

Bake at 350°F for 25 minutes or until toothpick test proves doneness. Serve warm with eggs for breakfast or brunch, or with soup and salad for lunch.

Mary K. White, Kennebunkport, ME

Blueberry Cheesecake Muffins

1 1/2 cups King Arthur Unbleached All-Purpose Flour
1/3 cup plus 2-3 tablespoons sugar (depending on tartness of the berries)
3 teaspoons baking powder
1/2 teaspoon salt
1/4 teaspoon almond extract
1/4 cup melted butter
1/3 cup plain yogurt
1/2 teaspoon vanilla extract
2/3 cup ricotta cheese
2 eggs
1 cup blueberries (mix these with a few tablespoons of the flour mixture)

Preheat oven to 375°F. Grease or paper-line 8-10 muffin tins. In a large bowl combine with a wire whisk the flour, sugar, baking powder and salt and whisk until well blended.

In a medium-sized bowl beat together the almond extract, melted butter, yogurt, vanilla, ricotta cheese and eggs, and add to flour mixture. Carefully fold in the blueberries. Batter will be soft and lumpy. Fill the muffin cups two-thirds full and bake 20 minutes.

Sandra Lucas Hurd, Southbury, CT

10

Here are the first- and second-prize recipes in the Muffins and Quick Breads category from the 1991 King Arthur Flour WinterBake: Savory Sausage Muffins and Blueberry Cheesecake Muffins, respectively.

JUNIOR YEAST BREADS & ROLLS

1st Prize
Easy Focaccia

3 cups King Arthur Unbleached All-Purpose Flour
1 1/2 teaspoons salt
1 tablespoon sugar
olive oil
2 tablespoons yeast dissolved in 1 cup lukewarm water
3 tablespoons tomato sauce
1 yellow onion, peeled and chopped
freshly cracked pepper

Mix flour, salt, sugar and 1/3 cup of olive oil in food processor. Mix thoroughly. Using the feed tube, add the yeast mixture to the flour mixture and process until dough forms a soft ball. Allow ball to rotate five times; let it rest for 10 minutes. Rotate five times more. Dough should be soft. Place dough in 1-quart bowl which has been well-oiled with olive oil. Cover and let rise in warm place 1 hour, or until doubled in bulk. Punch down.
On floured board, roll dough until it fits a 9x13-inch cookie sheet which has been well oiled with olive oil. Let rise 1/2 hour. Prick lightly several times with a fork. Lightly brush tomato sauce over top to achieve a slight taste of sauce. You should still be able to see the dough through the sauce. Sprinkle with olive oil, then sprinkle onions on the top. Generously sprinkle black pepper on the top; freshly ground works best.
Bake in the oven at 350°F for 20-25 minutes, or until light brown and firm. Slice into squares. Focaccia can be eaten hot, or cold as a basis for sandwiches. If you use for sandwiches, be sure to cut in half. Can also be used as basis for mini-pizzas.

Kate Easter, New Sweden, ME

2nd Prize
Cheesy Italian Dipping Rolls

1 package dry yeast
1 cup warm water
1/4 cup olive oil
2 tablespoons sugar
1 teaspoon salt
1 egg

3 cups King Arthur Unbleached Flour
4 ounces mozzarella cheese,
   cut into 10 3/4-inch cubes
3 tablespoons melted butter
2-3 tablespoons grated Parmesan cheese
fresh tomato sauce, warmed (optional)

Dissolve yeast in warm water. Add oil, sugar, salt, egg and half the flour. Stir until smooth; add the rest of the flour and blend in. Turn dough out onto a lightly floured board and knead lightly. Shape into 10 rolls, inserting one cube of cheese in center of each. Place rolls on greased cookie sheets away from draft. Let rise 1 hour. Brush each roll with melted butter and sprinkle with grated cheese. Bake at 375°F for 15-20 minutes, or until golden brown. Serve warm, dipped into tomato sauce if desired. Makes 10 rolls.

Michael Matino, Westfield, NJ

15

At the 1991 WinterBake, in the Junior Yeast Bread and Rolls category, the first prize went to the recipe for Easy Focaccia, and the second prize was awarded to Cheesy Italian Dipping Rolls.

1st Prize
Sourdough Parmesan Pesto Loaf

1 tablespoon dry yeast
3 tablespoons sugar
4 tablespoons warm tap water
1 cup sourdough starter
1 teaspoon salt
2 tablespoons cooking oil

3/4 cup warm milk
3 1/2 cups King Arthur Unbleached
   All-Purpose Flour
1 tablespoon butter or margarine, melted
2 tablespoons pesto sauce
3 tablespoons Parmesan cheese

Pour yeast, sugar, and tap water into a mixing bowl and allow yeast to dissolve. Add the sourdough starter, salt, cooking oil, and milk and mix well. Gradually add the flour, one cup at a time, and mix until the dough pulls away from the sides of the bowl. Turn dough out onto a floured surface and knead until smooth and elastic, about 5 minutes. Place dough into a greased bowl, turning once to coat the dough with the grease. Cover and let rise until doubled in bulk.
Punch down the dough, turn it out onto a floured surface and roll out to an 8x10-inch rectangle. Spread with the melted butter and the pesto sauce and sprinkle with the cheese. Roll up, beginning at the narrow side. Place into a greased loaf pan. Cover and let rise in a warm place until doubled in size. Bake at 350 F for 45-50 minutes. Remove from oven and cool 10 minutes before removing from pan. Serve hot or at room temperature. Makes 1 loaf.

Frances O'Connell, Los Angeles, CA

2nd Prize
Spinach Sourdough Sopaipillas

1 cup King Arthur Unbleached All-Purpose Flour
1 1/2 teaspoons baking powder
1 teaspoon garlic salt
1/8 teaspoon pepper
2 tablespoons shortening
1 cup sourdough starter
1 package (10 ounces) frozen chopped spinach, thawed and squeezed very dry
oil for frying
powdered sugar

In large bowl mix together flour, baking powder, garlic salt and pepper. Cut in shortening until mixture resembles cornmeal. Add sourdough starter and spinach. Stir quickly with a fork just until dry ingredients are moistened.
Turn out on floured surface and knead until smooth, adding flour if needed. Cover with dish towel and let dough rest 5 minutes. Heat oil to 400 F in deep pan. Roll dough into a 12x15-inch rectangle. Cut into 3-inch squares. Drop squares, a few at a time, into hot oil. Fry until golden brown, about 2 minutes on each side. Drain on paper towels. Serve warm, sprinkled with powdered sugar. Makes 4 servings.

Gloria T. Bove, Bethlehem, PA

18

In the 1991 WinterBake Sourdough category, first prize was awarded to the recipe for Sourdough Parmesan Pesto Loaf. Spinach Sourdough Sopaipillas took the second spot.

In the popular Pizza category, 1991 WinterBake winners were Pizza Pretzels and Appetizer Pizza.

1st Prize

Pizza Pretzels

3/4 cup diced smoked sausage	3/4 cup warm water
1/4 cup finely chopped bell pepper	1 tablespoon oil
1/4 cup finely chopped onion	1/2 teaspoon salt
1 cup shredded mozzarella cheese	2 to 2 1/2 cups King Arthur Unbleached Flour
1/2 cup pizza sauce	1 tablespoon melted butter
1/4 teaspoon sugar	2 tablespoons grated Parmesan cheese
1 package active dry yeast	1 teaspoon poppy seeds

Preheat oven to 400°F. Combine first five ingredients for filling. Mix well and set aside. Dissolve sugar and yeast in warm water. Add oil, salt and 2 cups of flour and stir well. Gradually add more flour to make a stiff dough. Turn the dough onto a floured surface and knead until smooth. Divide the dough into five equal portions. Roll each portion to a rectangle about 10x3 inches. Gently pull to a length of about 12 inches. Spoon about 1/3 cup of the filling down the center of each strip. Pull the dough upwards over the filling and pinch the edges to seal. Be sure that the filling is sealed well inside the dough. Gently pull and shape like large pretzels. Brush with melted butter and sprinkle with Parmesan and poppy seeds. Place pretzels on a greased baking sheet and bake for 18 to 20 minutes. Remove to a rack to cool slightly before eating.
Cooked, well-drained ground beef or pork sausage can be substituted for the smoked sausage.

Prudence Hilburn, Piedmont, AL

2nd Prize

Appetizer Pizza

1 package dry yeast	1/3 cup grated Romano cheese
1 1/2 teaspoons sugar	1 cup pesto sauce
1 1/2 cups lukewarm water	anchovies to taste
2 tablespoons olive oil	1 small (5 oz.) sweet dry Italian sausage
1 1/2 teaspoons salt	1/2 cup sliced black olives
4 1/4 cups King Arthur Unbleached Flour	1/2 cup diced marinated artichoke hearts
Topping:	1/3 cup chopped roasted peppers
3 whole unpeeled garlic bulbs	1/2 pound ricotta cheese
4 tablespoons olive oil (approx.)	

Dissolve yeast and sugar in water; let stand 10 minutes. Add oil and salt. With dough hooks, mix on low, adding flour slowly until soft ball forms. Knead with machine for 3 to 4 minutes. Knead by hand on lightly floured surface to a smooth ball. Place dough in a greased bowl (use olive oil). Cover and let stand until almost doubled. While dough is rising, place garlic on a baking sheet; drizzle 1 tablespoon oil on each bulb. Roast at 375°F until entire bulb is soft (20 minutes). Let sit until cool enough to handle. Remove the roasted cloves from the husks. Mash garlic into a paste. Punch down the dough. Stretch dough to fit a well-oiled 15-inch round deep pizza pan. Let rise 30 minutes. Preheat oven to 425°F. Brush pizza with olive oil, spread with garlic paste, and sprinkle with cheese. Bake 20 minutes. Remove from oven. Spread pesto sauce over pizza; arrange remaining toppings, except ricotta cheese, on pizza. Place teaspoon-sized dollops of ricotta cheese over top of pizza. Bake 10 to 15 minutes till bottom is light brown; let sit for 5 minutes before cutting. Cut in 1-inch wedges.

Sharon Ruggiero, Manchester, CT

21

1st Prize

Spinach Spaetzle

3 eggs	1 cup finely chopped fresh spinach
2/3 cup milk or water	3 tablespoons butter
2 cups King Arthur Unbleached Flour	salt
1/2 teaspoon baking powder	pepper
1/4 teaspoon salt	1/2 cup freshly grated Parmesan
1/4 teaspoon nutmeg	

Beat together eggs and milk. Combine dry ingredients in large bowl. Add egg mixture and blend until batter is smooth. Add chopped spinach. Let batter rest about 20 minutes.
Bring 4 quarts of water to a boil in a large pot. Place 1/2 of batter inside a spaetzle maker or colander with small holes. Push batter through holes into boiling water. Spaetzle will float to the surface when done. Strain and repeat with remaining batter.
Sauté spaetzle in a large frying pan with butter. Season with salt and pepper and Parmesan cheese. Spaetzle may be used to accompany stews or sauces, and in soups. Makes 4-6 servings.

Whitney Lamy, Salem, MA

2nd Prize

Black Pepper, Scallion, & Mushroom Pasta

2 cups King Arthur Unbleached Flour
3 large eggs
1 teaspoon freshly ground black pepper
2 large scallions, finely chopped
1/2 cup finely diced mushrooms. (squeezed dry)
1/2 teaspoon salt

In the work bowl of a food processor, put the flour, eggs, black pepper, scallions and mushrooms and process until consistency of small beads, about 2-3 minutes, using either the metal or plastic blades.
Press the beads of dough together to form a ball, wrap in plastic wrap, and let rest about half an hour or more. Roll out very thin, using a rolling pin or a pasta machine. Do not use number 7 notch, as that's a little too thin. Cut into 1/2 inch wide strips or by machine using fettucine cutter.
Bring 2 quarts of water to a boil and add salt. Cook pasta 2-4 minutes until done. Good served with pesto or tomato sauce, or butter and herbs. Makes 4-6 servings.

Pamela J. Mackay, Acushnet, MA

25

The 1991 WinterBake had a Homemade Pasta category. The first-prize winner was the recipe for Spinach Spaetzle. The second spot went to the recipe for Black Pepper, Scallion, and Mushroom Pasta from Acushnet, Massachusetts.

In the 1991 WinterBake category of Cookies & Bars, the first prize was awarded to the recipe for Pumpkin Maple Cookies. The recipe taking second was for Blueberry Mookies, which called for three quarters of a cup of blueberries (preferably wild).

1st prize

COOKIES & BARS

Pumpkin Maple Cookies

1/2 cup margarine or butter
1 1/2 cups brown sugar, packed
2 eggs
1 cup ricotta cheese
1 teaspoon maple flavoring
3/4 cup pumpkin puree

2 3/4 cups King Arthur Unbleached Flour
1 tablespoon baking powder
1/2 teaspoon baking soda
1 teaspoon salt
1 cup chopped walnuts

Cream butter or margarine and sugar. Add eggs and mix thoroughly. Stir in ricotta cheese, maple flavoring and pumpkin puree until well blended. Sift together flour, baking powder, soda, and salt and stir into egg mixture. Mix in walnuts. Chill if the dough is soft.
Drop rounded tablespoonfuls of dough about 2 inches apart on greased baking sheet. Bake at 375°F about 10 minutes or until no dent remains when cookies are touched lightly on top. Cool. Spread with and icing made with maple flavoring in place of vanilla. Makes about 4 dozen cookies.

Barbara L. Johnson, Monmouth, ME

2nd prize

Blueberry "Mookies"

4 ounces almond paste
1/2 cup sour cream
2 eggs, beaten
1/2 cup brown sugar
1/2 cup sugar
1/2 cup butter, room temperature
1/2 teaspoon salt
1/2 teaspoon baking soda
2 cups King Arthur Unbleached Flour
  (reserve 1/2 cup to dredge blueberries)
3/4 cup blueberries (preferably wild)
1/2 cup coconut

Preheat oven to 375°F. Cream the almond paste with sour cream. Add beaten eggs. Beat again. Add sugars, butter, and salt and beat well. Sift baking soda into flour and add to mix. Beat until smooth.
Dredge blueberries in remaining flour and, along with coconut, fold into dough. Place heaping teaspoons of batter 1 inch apart on greased baking sheets. Bake for 8 minutes, or until lightly browned. Remove and place cookies on wire rack to cool. Makes approximately 80 cookies.

* For other fruit variations try substituting 2 8-ounce cans, drained crushed pineapple or 3/4 to 1 cup, mashed banana instead of the blueberries.

Leonard Weiner, West Newton, MA

27

5th prize

Graham's Chocolate Chip Cinnamon Roll

1/3 cup sugar
5 tablespoons milk
2 teaspoons baking powder
1/2 cup confectioners' sugar
1 1/2 cups plus 2 tablespoons King Arthur
  Unbleached All-Purpose Flour
4 tablespoons melted butter
1 egg

5 teaspoons miniature chocolate chips
2 1/2 teaspoons dark brown sugar
1/2 teaspoon vanilla extract

Filling:
1 teaspoon cinnamon
3 tablespoons brown sugar
3/4 cup chopped pecans

Preheat oven to 350°F. Mix above ingredients with electric beater. On a floured board, knead and add flour until it's not sticky. Roll out with rolling pin to 1/4 to 1/2-inch thick.
Mix filling ingredients. Sprinkle 2/3 mixture over rolled-out dough. Roll up so you make a long roll. Slice about 1 inch thick, and sprinkle with remaining brown sugar-cinnamon-pecan mixture. Put on greased cookie sheet, and bake at 350°F for approximately 15 minutes, until golden brown.

Graham Connell, Warren, VT

CAKES & COBBLERS

1st prize

Cranberry Poppy Seed Pound Cake

1 cup unsalted butter, softened
2 cups sugar
4 large eggs, at room temperature
2 1/2 cups King Arthur Unbleached Flour
1 teaspoon baking powder
1/2 teaspoon baking soda
1/2 teaspoon salt
1 tablespoon ground ginger
1/3 cup evaporated milk
2 1/2 cups cranberries, picked over
1/2 cup poppy seeds

In a large bowl cream the butter, then add the sugar, a little at a time, while beating with electric mixer. Beat until fluffy. Add the eggs, one at a time, beating well after each egg. In another bowl, sift together the flour, baking powder, baking soda, salt and ginger. Add to the creamed mixture alternately with the milk. Fold in the cranberries and poppy seeds and spoon into a buttered and floured bundt pan. Bake at 350°F for 1 1/4 hours or until tester comes out clean. Cool for 10 minutes, then turn out onto rack. Makes 8-10 servings.

Pamela J. Mackay, Acushnet, MA

31

First prize in the 1991 WinterBake in the Cakes & Cobblers category, was awarded to the recipe for this delicious Cranberry Poppy Seed Pound Cake, sent in from Acushnet, Massachusetts.

Melissa's Cranberry Torte, using one and a half cups of King Arthur all-purpose flour, was awarded first prize in the Junior Cakes & Cobblers category at the 1991 WinterBake.

sugar and beat until they stand in soft peaks. Stir one-fourth of the whites into the yolk mixture. Spoon the remaining egg whites over the yolk mixture, sift the flour over the top of the whites, and fold gently all together to blend. Pour into prepared pan and bake for 30 minutes, until golden. Remove from oven, cool 10 minutes, then remove cake from pan. Cool completely.

With an electric mixer, beat the egg yolks and sugar until light in color. Pour in the boiling milk and beat until blended. Place this mixture in a saucepan and stir constantly over low heat until thick and smooth. Remove from heat and stir in vanilla. Cool. Soften the gelatin in the hot water and place over a pan of boiling water to dissolve completely. In a large bowl, place the ricotta cheese, rum, and coffee liqueur and stir. Add the cooled custard and slowly stir in the gelatin until well blended. Fold in the whipped cream.

Split the cake into two layers. Place the bottom half into the springform pan. Mix the espresso with the three tablespoons of coffee liqueur and sprinkle half this mixture over the cake in the pan. Pour the custard filling over the cake. Place the top layer of cake over the custard and sprinkle with the remaining coffee mixture. Cover with foil and chill four hours or overnight. Before serving, sift the cocoa over the top of the cake. Remove sides of pan, slice and serve.

Frances O'Connell, Los Angeles, CA

JUNIOR CAKES & COBBLERS

1st Prize — Melissa's Cranberry Torte

Filling:	Dough:
3/4 cup water	3/4 cup butter or margarine
1/2 cup sugar	3/4 cup sugar
1/2 cup honey	1 cup finely ground almonds
1 12-ounce bag of cranberries	1 1/2 cups King Arthur Unbleached Flour
1 tablespoon cornstarch	3/4 teaspoon cinnamon
1 tablespoon cold water	3/4 teaspoon cloves
grated rind of 1/2 orange	1 egg
	1 teaspoon cold water
	1 teaspoon sugar

Combine the water, sugar, and honey in a saucepan. Boil, stirring occasionally, for about 5 minutes. Chop cranberries roughly in a food processor. Add cranberries and orange rind to the mixture and simmer over low heat, without stirring, for 5 more minutes. Mix cornstarch and 1 tablespoon water. Add to cranberry mixture and cook over low heat for about 3 minutes, or until thick. Cool. Preheat the oven to 350°F. Beat butter and sugar until creamy. Add ground almonds. Sift flour and spices together and add to mixture. Butter a springform pan. Pat two-thirds of the dough on the bottom and sides of the pan, making sure the dough is steeper on the edges. Spread the cooled cranberry mixture over the dough. Roll out the rest of the dough on a lightly floured surface and cut into strips about 1 inch wide. Make a crisscross pattern with the strips on the torte, making sure they're pressed into the dough on the sides. Beat the egg with 1 teaspoon cold water and brush over the dough. Sprinkle with 1 teaspoon sugar. Bake for 40 minutes, or until brown on top. Cool, then gently remove the sides of the pan.

Melissa Tischler, Sudbury, MA

34

PIES & PASTRY

1st Prize — Chilled Cream Cheese And Salmon Tart

Crust (for one 9-inch pan):	
1 1/2 cups King Arthur Unbleached Flour	1 scallion, white part only, cut into small pieces
1/2 cup plus 2 tablespoons unsalted butter, chilled and cut into chunks	Pinch of white pepper
1 1/2 ounces cream cheese, cut into chunks	1/4 teaspoon celery salt
1/2 teaspoon salt	3/4 teaspoon dried dill
1/2 teaspoon dried dill	2 ounces smoked salmon
1 1/2 tablespoons vinegar	Garnish:
Filling:	Zucchini and radishes
2 8-ounce packages cream cheese, cut into small chunks	1 hard-boiled egg yolk, chopped
2 tablespoons plain yogurt	1/2 cup chopped parsley
	1 finely sliced scallion (white part only)

Place all ingredients for crust, except the vinegar into the work bowl of a food processor with a steel blade attached, and process with 3 or 4 bursts, until the mixture has the consistency of coarse meal. Slowly, with the machine running, add the vinegar. As soon as the dough forms a ball on the blades, stop the machine and remove the dough. Press dough into a 9-inch quiche pan with a removable bottom, and refrigerate for at least 30 minutes. Preheat oven to 400°F. Remove chilled dough and prick bottom and sides all over with a fork. Line pan with foil or waxed paper, fill with dried beans, rice, or pie weights, and bake for 12 minutes. Remove from oven and remove the paper and weights. Return to oven and continue baking for an additional 10 to 14 minutes, or until lightly browned. Cool completely. Place all filling ingredients in work bowl of a food processor with steel blade attached, and process until smooth and creamy. Spoon into baked crust. Slice zucchini and radish with the 1mm blade of processor and place slices in alternating concentric circles on top of filling. Place balance of ingredients, except chopped parsley, in center of tart. The chopped parsley is sprinkled evenly over the top of the tart. Refrigerate until the tart is set. This can be made a day or two in advance.

F. Walter Koneman, Bloomfield, NJ

2nd Prize — Norwegian Apple Pie

Crust:	2 teaspoons orange juice
1 cup King Arthur Unbleached Flour	1/8 teaspoon salt
1 teaspoon sugar	1/2 cup sour cream
1/4 teaspoon salt	5 medium Granny Smith apples, pared, peeled and sliced
1/3 cup shortening	Topping:
1 teaspoon white vinegar	1 cup sugar
1 large egg, beaten, at room temperature	1 cup plus 2 tablespoons King Arthur Unbleached Flour
Filling:	1 large egg, beaten
3/4 cup granulated sugar	3/4 cup melted butter, cooled
1/4 cup packed brown sugar	1/2 cup chopped pecans
2 tablespoons King Arthur Unbleached Flour	1/8 teaspoon salt
1/2 teaspoon cinnamon	
1/4 teaspoon nutmeg	

37

At the 1991 WinterBake in the Pies & Pastry category, first prize was awarded to this entry from Bloomfield, New Jersey, for a Chilled Cream Cheese and Salmon Tart.

101

Spinach, Bacon and Cheese Pie

2 3/4 cups King Arthur Unbleached Flour
1/4 cup butter, chilled
1 tablespoon vegetable oil
1/2 teaspoon salt
1/2 cup cold water (approx.)
2 pounds fresh spinach, cleaned

6 ounces chopped bacon
1 clove garlic, chopped fine
1/4 cup chopped fresh parsley
1 egg, slightly beaten
2/3 cup freshly grated Parmesan cheese
salt & pepper to taste

Combine flour and salt. Cut in butter until pieces are size of small peas. Gradually add oil, salt and water, mixing until mixture is moistened. Form dough into a ball. Wrap in waxed paper and chill for 1 hour. Cook spinach in water, drain, press out as much water as possible. Chop spinach and and set aside. Fry all but 1 tablespoon of bacon until crisp. Remove from pan and drain on a paper towel. Reserve 2 tablespoons of fat in pan and add garlic and cook over medium heat for 2 minutes. Add spinach and cook 2 minutes more. Remove from heat and stir in parsley, egg and cheese. Season with salt and pepper to taste. Roll out two-thirds of dough 1/4-inch thick to line a 9-inch pie pan. Spoon in filling. Roll out remaining dough into a circle large enough to cover bottom crust. Seal edges together with a little water and the tines of a fork. Trim edges. Cut steam holes or slits into top layer of dough. Sprinkle with rest of chopped bacon and bake in preheated 400°F oven for about 3/4 hour, until crust is lightly browned. Serve hot or cold.

Ralph Picarello, Paramus, NJ

100% WHOLE WHEAT

Whole Wheat Herb Bread

2 cups milk
1/4 cup margarine
2 tablespoons sugar
1 package yeast
2 cups King Arthur Whole Wheat Flour
1 teaspoon salt
1 1/2 teaspoons coarsely
ground black pepper

1 1/2 to 2 cups King Arthur Whole Wheat
 Flour
1 cup grated Cheddar cheese
1/2 cup chopped fresh parsley
1 tablespoon chopped fresh chives
2 teaspoons chopped fresh marjoram
2 teaspoons chopped fresh thyme
2 teaspoons chopped fresh basil

Scald milk. Add margarine and sugar. Stir until margarine melts. Let stand 5 minutes. Add yeast. Combine 2 cups flour, salt, and pepper with yeast mixture. Beat until smooth. Blend. Add remaining flour, as needed, to make a stiff dough. Knead till smooth and elastic. Place in greased bowl. Cover and let rise until double, 1 to 1 1/2 hours. Punch down. Turn out onto floured board and knead in cheese. Divide in half, cover and let rest 5 minutes. Roll each piece into a 15x9-inch rectangle. Combine fresh herbs and sprinkle on each. Roll up, jelly-roll fashion, starting at narrow end. Place seam side down in greased 9x5x3-inch loaf pans. Let rise, covered, in warm place until double, 45 to 60 minutes. Preheat oven to 350° F. Brush tops with melted butter or margarine. Bake at 350°F for 45 to 60 minutes.

Kathleen Hanning, W. Greenwich, RI

In the 100 percent Whole Wheat category at the 1991 WinterBake, first prize was earned for this recipe for Whole Wheat Herb Bread.

Reuben Pizza

Crust:
1 tablespoon or packet active dry yeast
1 cup warm water (110°F)
1 teaspoon sugar
1 1/2 tablespoons oil
1 clove garlic, pressed
1 1/2 tablespoons caraway seeds
1/2 teaspoon salt

3 cups King Arthur Unbleached All-Purpose Flour
olive oil to brush on crust
Topping:
1/2 pound grated swiss cheese
2 cups well-drained sauerkraut
1 pound sliced corned beef
1 pound grated mozzarella cheese
Freshly ground pepper

In a large bowl, dissolve yeast in warm water, add sugar and allow to stand for five minutes, until foamy. Add oil, garlic, caraway seeds and salt. Add flour one half cup at a time, stirring until dough begins to pull away from sides of the bowl. Knead dough on a floured board for 5-10 minutes, adding more flour as needed. Place dough in greased bowl, turning once to coat top. Cover with plastic wrap and allow dough to rise in a warm place for about 15 minutes. Do not allow dough to become over-light. When dough has risen, divide into two pieces, and roll each piece to fit a 12-inch round pizza pan, or a 13 x 9-inch rectangular pan. Form a small rim around the edge of the pizza. Place in greased pan, prick dough all over with a fork and allow to rise for another 15 minutes. Brush crust lightly with olive oil and bake in the middle of a preheated 400°F oven for about 10 minutes, or until lightly browned. Divide topping ingredients evenly between the two pizzas and place on top of crust in the following order: cheese, sauerkraut, corned beef, mozzarella and pepper. Bake for 10-20 minutes more, until cheese is bubbling. Serve immediately.

Emily Koch, Schenectady, NY

5

The overall grand prize at the 1993 WinterBake was awarded for this delicious Reuben Pizza recipe.

The Junior Grand Prize at the 1993 WinterBake was awarded to this recipe for Apple-Nut Coffee Cake.

Jr. Grand Prize | Apple-Nut Coffee Cake

1 cup King Arthur Unbleached All-Purpose Flour
1/2 teaspoon baking powder
1/2 teaspoon baking soda
1/8 teaspoon salt
1/2 cup sugar
1/4 cup shortening
1 egg
1/2 teaspoon vanilla
1 apple, cored and chopped
1/2 cup sour cream
1/4 cup walnuts, crushed
1/4 cup brown sugar
1 tablespoon butter
1/2 teaspoon cinnamon

Grease and flour an 8-inch round cake pan. In medium bowl stir together flour, baking powder, soda and salt. In large bowl beat together sugar and shortening until fluffy. Beat in egg and vanilla. Stir about half the flour mixture into the sugar mixture. Stir in sour cream. Stir in the rest of the flour mixture. Stir in apple and spread evenly into greased pan.
Put nuts, brown sugar, butter and cinnamon into a small bowl and mix until crumbly. Sprinkle over coffee cake. Bake in a 350 F oven for 25-30 minutes or until done. Serve warm.

Meghan Barron, Arnold, MD

PANCAKES, WAFFLES & CREPES

1st Prize | Muy Bueno Blintzes

Crepe:
1/4 cup cornmeal
3/4 cup King Arthur Unbleached Flour
1 teaspoon sugar
1/2 teaspoon baking soda
1/8 teaspoon salt
1 1/2 cups milk
1 egg
1/2 cup butter
Filling:
3 tablespoons olive oil

1 clove garlic
3/4 cup onion, chopped
1/2 cup bell pepper, chopped
1 cup black beans
1/2 cup cooked corn, fresh or canned
1/4 cup medium hot salsa
1/4 cup cilantro, chopped
salt and pepper to taste
1/4 cup cheddar cheese, shredded
garnish with additional chopped cilantro

For the crepes: In a medium sized bowl combine cornmeal, flour, sugar, baking soda and salt. Melt 4 tablespoons of butter and add to dry mixture along with the milk and egg. Mix well. Refrigerate for 45 minutes. Heat 1 teaspoon of butter in an 8-inch crepe pan over medium heat. Pour a scant 1/4 cup of batter into the pan and tip pan to coat the bottom. Cook for 2 minutes or until the bottom is golden and the top is set. Loosen and flip crepe using a spatula. Cook for 45 seconds. Slip crepe onto waxed paper. Repeat for each crepe using butter in the pan each time. May be made ahead and refrigerated.
For the batter: Heat oil in medium skillet over medium heat. Saute garlic, onion and pepper for 5 minutes. Add beans, corn, salsa, cilantro and season with salt and pepper to taste.
To assemble and bake: Spread 2-3 tablespoons of filling on each crepe and spread to within 1/2 inch of edge; fold two sides of the crepe slightly towards the center then roll in opposite direction, jelly roll style. Preheat oven to 350°F. In a 9 x 12 inch pan melt remaining butter. Remove pan from oven. Arrange crepes in one layer, sprinkle with cheese and bake 15 minutes or until heated through. Garnish with chopped cilantro and pass additional salsa if desired. Serves 4 main course or 8 appetizers.

Lois Rosen, Los Angeles, CA

2nd Prize | Peaches and Cream Pancakes

1 egg, separated
1/2 cup heavy or whipping cream
3 tablespoons butter, melted
1 teaspoon vanilla
1/2 cup King Arthur Unbleached All-Purpose Flour
1/2 teaspoon baking powder
1 tablespoon sugar
1/2 cup chopped peaches

Beat egg yolk until light. Beat in cream, butter, and vanilla. Combine flour, baking powder and sugar and blend into egg yolk mixture. Beat egg whites until stiff and fold into batter. Carefully fold peaches into batter. Heat griddle. Use scant 1/4 cup for each pancake. Cook batter until first side puffs and bubbles and then turn. Continue cooking 1 minute more or until done. This batter also works in a waffle iron.

Kathleen Hanning, West Greenwich, RI

7

The 1993 WinterBake had a Pancakes, Waffles & Crepes category. Top honors went to Muy Bueno Blintzes, from a contestant in Los Angeles. In second, it was Peaches and Cream Pancakes.

YEAST BREADS AND ROLLS

1st Prize
Crunchy Seasoned Pull-Apart Bread

1/2 cup hot tap water (approx. 105°F)	1 1/2 cups hot tap water
1 tablespoon sugar	5 1/2 to 6 cups King Arthur Unbleached Flour
1 pinch ginger	*Seasoning:*
1 tablespoon or packet active dry yeast	4 tablespoons grated parmesan cheese
2 teaspoons salt	2 tablespoons grated romano cheese
2 tablespoons olive oil	4 teaspoons chopped basil

In a large mixing bowl, combine water, sugar, ginger and yeast. Let stand 5 minutes until yeast is frothy; stir to blend. With electric mixer on low speed add salt, oil, hot water and 2 cups flour. Mix until well blended and smooth - change to dough hooks on mixer. Add 2 more cups of flour using highest speed, scraping bowl with spatula occasionally. Add additional flour 1/2 cup at a time until dough pulls up into a ball and is still a little tacky to the touch. Turn into a lightly oiled bowl turning to coat on all sides. Cover and let rise until double in bulk.

Combine seasoning ingredients in a small bowl. When dough has risen - punch down - spray two bundt-style pans with non-stick vegetable spray. Cut the dough into pieces small enough to be about the size of a large walnut. - put olive oil on hands and roll pieces into a ball. Then roll in seasoning mixture and place side by side in pan making two layers. Set aside and allow to rise until almost doubled again. Preheat oven to 400°F while loaves are rising. When thoroughly risen bake for approximately 20-25 minutes until tops are golden. Turn out onto cooling racks or serve immediately.

Theresa Militello, Brockport, NY

2nd Prize
Raspberry Cheese Breakfast Rolls

Dough:	1 egg, beaten
1 tablespoon or packet active dry yeast	2 1/2 to 3 cups King Arthur Unbleached Flour
1/2 cup warm water	
2 tablespoons sugar	*Filling:*
1/2 cup milk, scalded	6 ounces cream cheese, softened
2 tablespoons butter	1/2 cup sugar
1 teaspoon salt	2 cups frozen raspberries

In a large bowl dissolve yeast in warm water. Sprinkle 2 tablespoons of sugar on top and let stand. To scalded milk add butter and salt. Let butter melt and allow milk to cool down to temperature of water. Add milk mixture and beaten egg to yeast mixture. Stir in 2 cups of flour. Add enough additional flour to make dough smooth and elastic. Knead on floured surface for 5 minutes. Place dough in lightly oiled bowl, turning once to coat the top. Cover and let rise for 1 hour. Beat together softened cream cheese and 1/2 cup sugar. Roll dough into a 10" x 16" rectangle. Carefully spread cream cheese mixture onto dough making sure to reach all edges. Sprinkle on frozen (fresh when in season) raspberries; gently press berries into cheese. Roll up beginning with 16-inch side. Carefully slice into 16 1-inch rolls. Place 8 rolls each into 2 well greased 8-inch round cake pans. Allow to rise for 1/2 hour. Bake for 35 minutes in an oven preheated to 350°F. Remove to platter and serve warm. *Nice with a simple icing drizzled over rolls!*

Abi Kibbe, Watertown, WI

In the 1993 WinterBake Yeast Breads and Rolls category, first prize was awarded for Crunchy Seasoned Pull-Apart Bread. The second spot went to a Wisconsin entrant for Raspberry Cheese Breakfast Rolls.

MUFFINS & QUICK BREADS

1st Prize
Sunshine Bread

3/4 cup dried apricots, chopped fine	2 1/2 teaspoons baking powder
1/2 cup boiling water	1/2 teaspoon baking soda
1 stick butter	1 cup almonds, chopped
1 cup sugar	1 tablespoon orange rind
2 beaten eggs	3/4 cup orange juice
2 cups King Arthur Unbleached Flour, sifted	*Topping:*
3/4 cup quick rolled oats, uncooked	2 tablespoons sugar
1/2 teaspoon salt	juice from 1/2 orange

In a saucepan, soak apricots in boiling water, cover and let stand for 1/2 hour. In large bowl, cream butter and sugar until fluffy. Add eggs, beat well. Stir in apricots, almonds and orange rind. Combine flour, oats, salt, baking powder and baking soda. Add flour mixture alternately with orange juice to creamed mixture, beginning and ending with dry ingredients. Pour into two greased and floured 9" loaf pans or one 13" loaf pan. Bake at 350°F for one hour. Brush with topping and let cool.

Mary Fenci, E. Sandwich, MA

2nd Prize
Sour Cream Scones

3 cups King Arthur Unbleached Flour	1/2 cup butter
3 teaspoons baking powder	3/4 cup dried currants or raisins
3 tablespoons sugar	1/2 cup sour cream
1/2 teaspoon baking soda	1 cup buttermilk
1 teaspoon salt	2 - 3 tablespoons heavy cream

In a large bowl, combine flour, baking powder, sugar, baking soda, and salt. Cut in butter until the mixture resembles coarse meal. Add currants, sour cream, and buttermilk. Mix until dough clings together. Turn dough out onto lightly floured board and roll to half-inch thickness. Using 2 1/2 or 3 inch cookie cutter, cut scones and place on a greased or parchment paper lined cookie sheet. Brush tops of scones with heavy cream and bake in a 425°F oven for 12-15 minutes. Serve warm with butter and jam.

Frances O'Connell, Los Angeles, CA

3rd Prize
Nell's Irish Bread

1 cup raisins	1/4 teaspoon baking soda
1/2 cup currants	1 cup shortening
4 1/2 cups King Arthur Unbleached Flour	2 eggs
1 cup sugar	2 cups milk (scant)
5 teaspoons baking powder	1/2 cup orange marmalade
1 1/2 teaspoons salt	1 tablespoon caraway seeds

Plump raisins in hot water 2-3 minutes, strain and set aside. (A couple of tablespoons of sherry or whisky can be added to the hot water). Mix all dry ingredients in a large mixing bowl. Cut in shortening with dry ingredients. In a smaller bowl beat eggs lightly, add milk and marmalade, mix well. Combine egg mixture with dry ingredients and beat well. Add raisins and currants, stir. Sprinkle top with caraway seeds and bake for 1 hour in a preheated 325°F oven, in a greased 10-inch cast iron frying pan or two 9"x5" loaf pans.

Susan Skiparis, Cheshire, CT

14

The top three spots in the 1993 WinterBake category for Muffins & Quick Breads went to Sunshine Bread, Sour Cream Scones, and Nell's Irish Bread, respectively.

Winners in the 1993 WinterBake Sourdough category were Sourdough Pecan Pumpkin Bread, submitted from Schenectady, New York, and Sourdough Coffee Cake, from Bridgton, Maine.

SOURDOUGH

1st Prize — Sourdough Pecan Pumpkin Bread

Sponge:
1/2 cup sourdough starter
1/2 cup buttermilk
1 cup King Arthur Unbleached Flour
Dough:
1 large egg
1/2 cup brownulated sugar
1 teaspoon vanilla extract
1/4 cup cooking oil
1/2 cup mashed cooked pumpkin
1 cup King Arthur Unbleached Flour

1/4 teaspoon salt
1 1/4 teaspoons baking soda
1 teaspoon cinnamon
1/2 teaspoon cloves
1 cup pecan halves (reserve 12 for topping)
2 large egg whites, beaten (reserve 3 tablespoons, beaten, for the topping)

Topping:
1/2 tablespoon granulated sugar
1/2 teaspoon cinnamon

Make a sponge of sourdough starter, warm buttermilk (110°F) and 1 cup King Arthur Unbleached All-Purpose Flour. Leave the sponge in a warm place (85°F) overnight. Add to the sponge: the egg, brownulated sugar, vanilla extract, oil and mashed pumpkin. Beat until smooth. Combine dry ingredients (additional cup of flour, salt, baking soda, cinnamon and cloves) and stir them into the sponge mixture. Reserve 12 pecan halves for topping. Break the rest of the pecans into pieces and add to the dough. Beat the egg whites until stiff, but not dry. Reserve 3 tablespoons of beaten egg whites for topping. Fold the rest of the egg whites into the mixture. Place the dough in greased loaf pan (9 x 5 x 3 inch), pushing the dough into the corners. For well-rounded loaf, leave dough in pan for 15 minutes before baking. Bake in center of preheated 350°F oven for 40 minutes. Paint top of bread with reserved beaten egg whites. Press reserved pecan halves on top, and sprinkle with mixture of granulated sugar and cinnamon. Continue baking for 15 minutes, or until a toothpick in center of bread comes out clean. Cool on a wire rack.

Emily Koch, Schenectady, NY

2nd Prize — Sourdough Coffee Cake

Batter:
1 cup sourdough starter
1 cup King Arthur Unbleached Flour
3/4 teaspoon baking soda
1/2 teaspoon salt
3/4 cup sugar
1/2 teaspoon cinnamon
1 egg, slightly beaten

1/3 cup vegetable oil
1/2 cup each chopped pecans and raisins

Topping:
1 cup sugar
2 tablespoons flour
1 tablespoon cinnamon
1/2 cup butter or margarine

Mix batter ingredients until smooth. Add nuts and/or dried fruit. Pour into two greased 8-inch pans square or round. It will scantily cover the bottom of the pans. Mix topping until blended and cover pastry with bits of topping. It will be almost covered completely. Bake at 350°F for 30 to 35 minutes. Tastes great!

Note: Other nuts such as walnuts are equally good. As for fruit, chopped dates, chopped prunes, dried apricot pieces and blueberries all make the cake good. Use your imagination - or what is at hand.

Shirley Chalken, Bridgton, ME

5th Prize — Chocolate Ravioli Drenched In Espresso Fudge Sauce

1 large egg, beaten
1 tablespoon water
1/2 teaspoon vanilla
3 tablespoons sugar
1/4 cup unsweetened cocoa
1 cup King Arthur Unbleached Flour
Almond filling:
1 8 ounce package cream cheese, softened
1/2 cup almonds, finely crushed
3 tablespoons sugar
1 teaspoon vanilla

Espresso fudge sauce:
1 cup sugar
2 tablespoons King Arthur Unbleached Flour
1/2 cup cold strong coffee
2 ounces (squares) unsweetened chocolate
2 tablespoons butter
1 teaspoon vanilla

1/2 cup chocolate covered espresso beans
2 cups sweetened whipped cream or topping
6 maraschino cherries, drained

Place first 4 ingredients into food processor. Using metal cutting blade process until sugar is dissolved. Add cocoa and flour; process until mixture leaves side of bowl. Add extra tablespoon of water if necessary and continue to process. Form into ball and let rest 20 minutes. Roll dough to desired thickness using pasta machine. Prepare to make ravioli according to directions for ravioli press. Combine filling ingredients until well-blended. Place teaspoon of almond filling on pasta. Insert a chocolate covered espresso bean into filling. Cover filling and finish making ravioli. Makes 36 two-inch ravioli. Cover and refrigerate until shortly before serving. To make sauce, combine first 4 ingredients in small saucepan. Cook and stir over medium heat until mixture bubbles and thickens. Remove from heat. Stir in butter and vanilla. Cook ravioli 4 minutes in large pot of slightly salted boiling water, stirring gently several times. Drain. Arrange ravioli on 6 dessert plates. Spoon warm espresso fudge sauce over ravioli. Place dollop of whipped cream on top andtop with a cherry.

Lois Dowling, Tacoma, WA

COOKIES AND BARS

1st Prize — Maple Walnut Spice Biscotti

2 large eggs
1/2 cup sugar
1/2 cup brown sugar
1/4 cup pure maple syrup
grated rind of one lemon

1/3 cup vegetable shortening, melted
2 1/2 cups King Arthur Unbleached Flour
2 teaspoons baking powder
1 teaspoon each ground cloves & cinnamon
2 cups walnuts, toasted

Preheat oven to 350°F. In large mixing bowl beat together eggs, sugars, maple syrup, lemon rind, and shortening. Add flour, baking powder and spices; mix well. Mix in nuts. Remove dough from mixing bowl and place on lightly floured surface. Divide dough into two equal pieces. Working with one piece at a time, flatten dough with hands and shape into an oval, approx. 10 inches long by 4 inches at its widest part in the center (the top and bottom will be narrower than the middle). Transfer oval onto greased cookie sheet. Repeat with other half of dough. Bake for 30 minutes. Remove from oven. Carefully transfer one oval cookie at a time to a cutting surface and slice 1" wide biscotti, on the diagonal, using a sharp, serrated knife. Repeat with other oval cookie. Return sliced cookies to cookie sheet, resting on their sides. They can be placed very close together. Bake 12 minutes. Remove from oven, turn on other side and bake 12 minutes more.

Lisa Hachey, Hopkinton, MA

25

From Tacoma, Washington, the Chocolate Ravioli Drenched in Espresso Fudge Sauce recipe used King Arthur all-purpose flour for the raviolis and in the fudge sauce. The first-place winner, Maple Walnut Spice Biscotti (in the Cookies and Bars category) was submitted by a Hopkinton, Massachusetts, resident.

🌾🌾🌾
WHOLE GRAIN

1st Prize — Spicy Wheat Banana Bread

1 cup mashed bananas (2-3)	1 cup old fashioned oats
1/2 cup dark molasses	1 tablespoon baking powder
1 cup buttermilk	1 teaspoon baking soda
2 eggs	2 teaspoons ground cinnamon
1/2 cup dark brown sugar	1 teaspoon each ground allspice and nutmeg
2 cups King Arthur Whole Wheat Flour	1 cup raisins

Preheat oven to 350°F. Mash the bananas. Stir in molasses, buttermilk and eggs. Add brown sugar and blend smooth. Add dry ingredients, mixing only enough to blend. Add raisins. Pour into two lightly greased loaf pans. Bake 40-50 minutes. Makes two loaves.

Kathleen Hanning, West Greenwich, RI

2nd Prize — Brickle Cinnamon Buns

Dough:

1/4 cup lukewarm water	1 teaspoon vanilla extract
1 tablespoon or packet active dry yeast	1 cup King Arthur Whole Wheat Flour
1/2 cup sugar	2 1/2 cups King Arthur Unbleached Flour
1/2 cup unsalted butter or margarine, softened	
2 eggs lightly beaten	**Filling:**
1/2 cup plain yogurt	1/4 cup sugar
1/2 teaspoon salt	2 tablespoons cinnamon
	2/3 - 1 cup each almond brickle chips and pecans

Proof yeast in the lukewarm water with 1 tablespoon sugar for 10 minutes. In a large mixing bowl, cream the butter with the remaining sugar. Stir in the eggs, yogurt, salt and vanilla. Add the yeast mixture. Stir in the whole wheat flour and 1 cup of the unbleached flour and beat well. Add the remaining 1 1/2 cups of flour a little bit at a time until the dough begins to pull away from the sides of the bowl. The dough should be quite sticky. Scrape down the sides of the bowl and cover with plastic wrap; refrigerate overnight. The following day, remove the dough from the refrigerator and scrape it out of the bowl onto a well floured board. Knead for 2 minutes.

Roll out dough on a lightly floured board into a 10-by-15-inch rectangle. Mix together the sugar and cinnamon and sprinkle them on to the dough, then sprinkle on the nuts and brickle. Starting with a long side, roll up jelly-roll fashion. Be sure to keep the roll tight. Slice the roll crosswise in 1 inch pieces. Place the slices in well greased cake pans, being sure to leave enough room for each slice to double in bulk. Makes 2 to 3 pans depending on their size. Cover with plastic wrap until doubled in bulk, 1 1/2 to 2 hours.

Bake in a preheated 350°F oven for 15 to 20 minutes, until golden brown. Cool on a wire rack. Serve warm.

Ann Lord, South Sutton, NH

38

The 1993 WinterBake featured a Whole Grain category. First prize was a recipe for Spicy Wheat Banana Bread, which used two cups of King Arthur whole-wheat flour. Second prize was awarded to a recipe for Brickle Cinnamon Buns, in which both King Arthur whole wheat and all-purpose flours are used.

WinterBake judge, Julia Child, is perhaps best known for her PBS television series, "The French Chef," "Julia Child and Company", and "Dinner at Julia's". She has authored and co-authored numerous cookbooks, and in 1989 her large, new, best-selling basic book, "The Way to Cook" was published by Alfred A. Knopf, Inc. She is very much committed not only to the furthering of gastronomy as a recognized discipline, but to the encouragement among young people to enter the profession. To this end she is an active member of the International Association of Culinary Professionals, and is particularly involved with "The American Institute of Wine and Food", of which she is one of the founders.

Julia Child's Focaccia
Italian Style Fresh Bread with Oil, etc.

Dough:
1 tablespoon or packet active dry yeast
1 tablespoon King Arthur Unbleached Flour
1 cup water
3 1/2 cups King Arthur Unbleached Flour
1 teaspoon salt
1 teaspoon Italian herb mixture or other dried herbs such as savory, thyme, oregano
1/4 cup fruity olive oil
Additional water as needed
Topping:
1 or 2 large cloves of garlic
1/4 teaspoon salt
3 tablespoons olive oil
2 to 3 tablespoons coarse or Kosher salt
Special Equipment Suggested: A food processor; a fairly straight-sided 4-quart bowl for dough rising; 2 lightly oiled baking sheets about 10 by 18-inches; a pastry brush

Julia Child

Blend the yeast, tablespoon of flour, and water in a 2-cup measure and let sit for several minutes until it foams. Measure 3 1/2 cups of flour, salt, and herbs into the bowl of the processor. Turn on the machine and slowly pour in the yeast, then the olive oil. If the dough does not form a ball in a few seconds, dribble in a little more water and continue with dribbles just until the dough forms a ball. Let the ball of dough rotate 8 to 10 times then feel it — if too soft and sticky, sprinkle on a tablespoon of flour and process a few seconds more, repeating if necessary. If mixture is stiff and hard, process in more droplets of water. Give dough a 3-minute rest, then continue processing, letting the ball rotate under the cover 30 more times. Turn dough out onto a lightly floured surface and let it rest 2 minutes. Then knead vigorously — folding it over on itself, and pushing it out with the heels of your hand, rapidly and vigorously, repeat the motion 30 to 40 times. The final dough should be smooth and elastic. Let rise about 1 1/2 hours or more. Turn the dough into the clean dry rising bowl. Cover the top of the bowl with plastic wrap, until the dough rise to almost triple its volume at a temperature of 70 to 75 F.

Preheat the oven to 450 F well before baking. Turn dough out onto lightly floured work surface; cut in half, and place one half on each baking sheet. Push each into a rough oval — the dough will soon resist you. Let it relax a few minutes while you prepare the topping, then continue, resting several minutes as necessary. You're aiming to achieve a rough, uneven, free-form oval-rectangular shape about 12" long and less than 1/2" thick. Then use your fingers to make 3 or 4 uneven indentations in the dough, and proceed at once to the topping — the dough is to rise as little as possible before baking.

Purée the garlic and mash to a paste with the table salt, then blend with the olive oil. Paint the mixture over the surface of the dough, sprinkle on the herbs and a generous amount of coarse salt. Bake 20 until lightly browned on top and bottom. They are at their very best freshly made and served while still warm. Makes two 9"x12" flat breads. For boutique-type focaccia, press into the formed dough such items as pungent chopped olives, sun-dried tomatoes, artichoke hearts, sausage or cheese bits.

41

Julia Child, well known for her PBS television series *The French Chef, Julia Child and Company,* and *Dinner at Julia's,* was one of the 1993 King Arthur WinterBake judges. She contributed her own wonderful focaccia recipe to the event's book.

Five

PACKAGING

The beautiful emblem of a knight on horseback has been the primary image of the company since 1896, when King Arthur Flour was first created. From turn-of-the-century flour barrels to today's flour packaging, the King Arthur logo takes center stage and immediately communicates the company's values: purity, loyalty, honesty, superior strength, and a dedication to a higher purpose.

From 1896 to today, the King Arthur emblem has been one of America's most recognizable logos.

Before the 1930s, flour was sold in barrels. With the development of cloth bags, transportation was made easier, even though the initial common size was a hefty 98 pounds.

Frank E. Sands, president, poses in the King Arthur Flour offices in the 1970s with a barrel once used to transport the company's flour.

Sands, Taylor & Wood offered many brands of flour exclusively for the bakery business. These work-of-art package designs were for Round Table Pastry Flour, Queen Guinevere Cake Flour, and Excalibur Flour. Today, the King Arthur Flour Company features nine different flours through its Bakery Food Service division.

King Arthur Coffee was offered starting in 1930. In Somerville, Massachusetts, at the King Arthur Flour offices, two employees in one room operated machinery to grind, pack, and seal coffee in vacuum-sealed glass jars. Coffee sold well for the company until rationing started during World War II (sales went from 38,489 jars sold in 1932 to 130,685 sold in 1942). After the war, King Arthur's coffee division operated again but not as successfully as during the 1930s. It was finally concluded in the 1970s.

In 1939, King Arthur Flour was sold along with coffee, tea, and wheat germ. In 1941, the company introduced biscuit mix. These products, other than flour, were eventually discontinued during World War II.

After barrels, cloth bags and paper bags served as the packaging for King Arthur Flour. At first, paper bags were tied at the top with a cord, as seen in this photograph taken when the King Arthur line included coffee and tea.

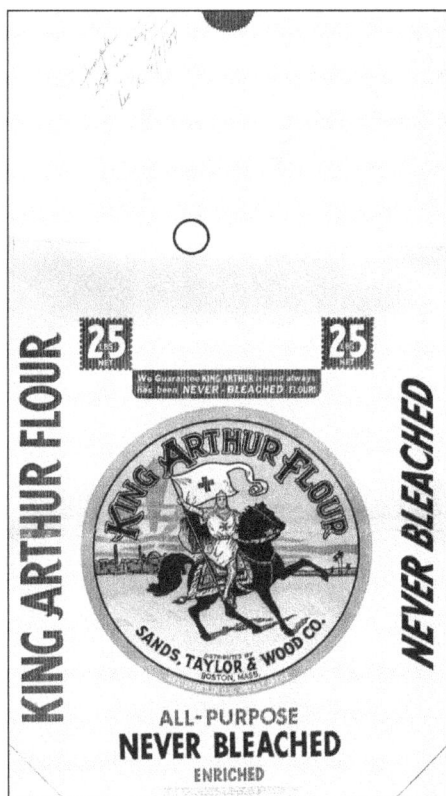

King Arthur Flour paper bags went from being tied at the top with a cord to being sealed with glue, a process still used today.

Later packaging for coffee was in round tin cans featuring beautiful artwork.

King Arthur Flour packaging always features the intrepid knight on horseback, along with important messages, such as "Never Bleached, Never Bromated."

King Arthur multipurpose white wheat flour was initially sold in stores starting in 1993. It provides all the nutrients of whole-wheat flour, with a lighter taste and color. It is referred to today as 100 percent white whole-wheat flour.

King Arthur white whole-wheat flour is used by many bakeries. Ideal uses include rolls, pizzas, tortillas, pita bread, muffins, brownies, and cookies.

King Arthur® Flour TV Ad Campaign Covers Entire U.S.!

Employee owned - committed to quality

UNBLEACHED
ALL-PURPOSE
FLOUR
America's highest grade since
Never Bleached •

Norwich, Vermont • www.kingarthurflour.com

King Arthur® Flour National Food Network TV Advertising Campaign, October 21 - December 1, 2003.

Over 100 prime 30-second commercials reaching over 81 million coast-to-coast FoodTV viewers!

Plus sponsorships and FoodTV.com!

Program	Spot Total	Highlights
M-F, 4 pm - 6 pm	28	Units to air "In the Kitchen" block
M-F, 4 pm - 6 pm	1	
M-F, 4 pm - 6 pm	6	Sponsorship of Paula's Home Cooking - 3 Billboards included
M-F, 4 pm - 6 pm	6	Program specific to "How to Boil Water" - Cooking for Beginners
M-F, 7 pm - 8 pm	15	Sponsorship of Sara's Secrets - 7 sponsorships, 2 spots and 1 billboard per sponsorship
M-SU, 8 pm - 1 am	3	Emeril Lagasse Live Combo
M-SU, 8 pm - 12 am	38	Prime Wheel - 19 units will air 8 pm - 12 am, 19 will repeat at 12 am - 38 units total
M-SU, 9 pm - 11 pm	1	Food Network Special
M-SU, 9 am - 2 pm	12	Food Network's "In the Kitchen" block
SA, 9 am - 8 pm	9	Special FoodTV Shows - Female Audience

TOTAL COMMERCIALS: 119!!

Employee Owned • Committed to Quality • www.kingarthurflour.com

Today, King Arthur Flour Company packaging can be seen on store shelves in all 50 states. It is a popular flour of choice for America's top bakers and chefs. The packaging is often seen on popular television cooking shows.

Is there an empty space deep within you?
Is it shaped like a scone?

King Arthur® Flour NEW MIXES FSI Out October 5th!

The new all natural mixes from King Arthur Flour

$1 OFF KING ARTHUR FLOUR MIXES

Newspapers and Circulation on back!

Employee Owned • Committed to Quality
www.kingarthurflour.com

© The King Arthur Flour Company, Inc. - 2004

In 2003, the King Arthur Flour Company introduced new all-natural quick mixes. The mixes were initially sold in New England and the western United States, and after immediate success, they quickly expanded to other parts of the country.

Six

THE EMPLOYEE OWNERSHIP ERA

After more than two centuries in business, the King Arthur Flour Company in 1996 began the Employee Stock Ownership Plan (ESOP). Embracing a team approach to management, the change to employee ownership helped attract highly qualified, motivated, and productive people, who empower each other and therefore strengthen the entire company. The plan resulted in 100 percent employee ownership of the King Arthur Flour Company in 2004.

Since becoming employee owned, the King Arthur Flour Company has reached several important milestones, including increasing the number of states King Arthur Flour is sold in from 11 to 50; becoming the third bestselling flour in the United States and the No. 1 top-selling whole-wheat flour overall; publishing *The Baker's Companion,* which won the James Beard Award for best cookbook of the year; and adding all-natural quick mixes and organic flours to the retail line.

A new timber-frame headquarters named Camelot was built in Norwich, Vermont, in 1995. In addition to being the main offices for the employees of the King Arthur Flour Company, Camelot is home to Vermont Public Radio.

Camelot is seen under construction. The headquarters measures 16,600 square feet. In 2004, the Baker's Store opened on the first level.

Camelot is in the early stages of construction in these photographs.

Brinna and Frank E. Sands II are shown here in 1997.

Chairman of the board Frank E. Sands II (left) is shown with King Arthur Flour Company president Steve Voigt.

The King Arthur Flour Company communicates its employee ownership in a variety of places. On flour bags, for example, "Employee owned, committed to quality," is proudly displayed across the top.

Thank you VBM!

We're honored to be part of your 5x5x5 Awards!

From the Employee Owners at The King Arthur Flour Company, Inc.

When the King Arthur Flour Company received an award from *Vermont Business* magazine, the thank-you advertisement came from the employee owners.

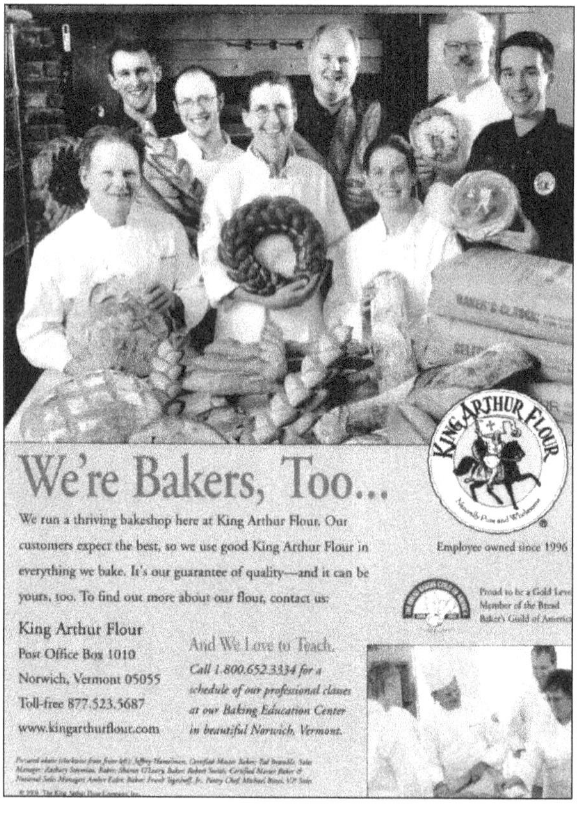

We're Bakers, Too...
We run a thriving bakeshop here at King Arthur Flour. Our customers expect the best, so we use good King Arthur Flour in everything we bake. It's our guarantee of quality—and it can be yours, too. To find out more about our flour, contact us:
King Arthur Flour
Post Office Box 1010
Norwich, Vermont 05055
Toll-free 877.523.5687
www.kingarthurflour.com
And We Love to Teach.
Call 1.800.652.3334 for a schedule of our professional classes at our Baking Education Center in beautiful Norwich, Vermont.
KING ARTHUR FLOUR
Employee owned since 1996

Company advertising reflects King Arthur's employee ownership. In this popular 2004 advertisement, employees from different parts of the company gather to display breads made in the Norwich bakery.

The employees of the King Arthur Flour Company show their owner status in a variety of ways: on their cars, Christmas trees, and even in music on a special holiday CD.

This commemorative Christmas ornament is another example of how the King Arthur Flour Company celebrates its employee ownership.

In 1998, King Arthur celebrated the holidays with a greatest hits album featuring employee artists singing "Twenty-one Trucks and Dozen Roses" and "King Arthur Doesn't Live Here Anymore," among other hits.

Recipe for Ownership

Ingredients:

2 Centuries of history as America's oldest flour company
1 ESOP (Employee Stock Ownership Plan)
Roughly 160 Employee-Owners, prepared well
5 King Arthur Family Flours (Supermarket Flours)
8 King Arthur Bakery Flours
1 Baker's Catalogue
1 Baker's Store
1 Fulfillment Center
1 King Arthur Flour Bakery
1 King Arthur Flour Baking Education Center
1 kingarthurflour.com Web site

Mix employee-owners into Family Flour, Bakery Flour, Baker's Catalogue, Baker's Store, Fulfillment Center, Bakery, Baking Education Center and Web site. Using teamwork, blend together vigorously, forming a cohesive mass.

Place on top of history, fold in the ESOP, and allow to grow.

Bake for several years. Best served with excellence and enthusiasm.

The King Arthur Flour Company, Inc.   2003

Posted in different locations around the company offices is the Recipe for Ownership, a fun way to communicate the special nature of employee ownership.

In 1996, the company started its employee ownership plan. In 2004, it became 100 percent employee owned.

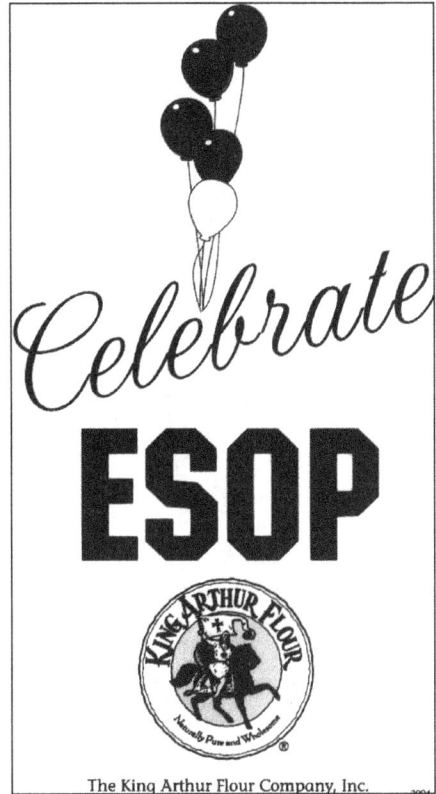

Celebrate

ESOP

The King Arthur Flour Company, Inc.

THE
KING ARTHUR FLOUR
BAKER'S CATALOGUE

Norwich, Vermont $2.00

King Arthur Flour's *The Baker's Catalogue* started in 1990. The company's 35,000-square-foot warehouse, named Avalon, was built in 1998. Avalon was expanded in 2004. Today, the company sends out more than eight million catalogs annually.

Shown here is the winter–early spring edition of *The Baker's Catalogue* from 1995.

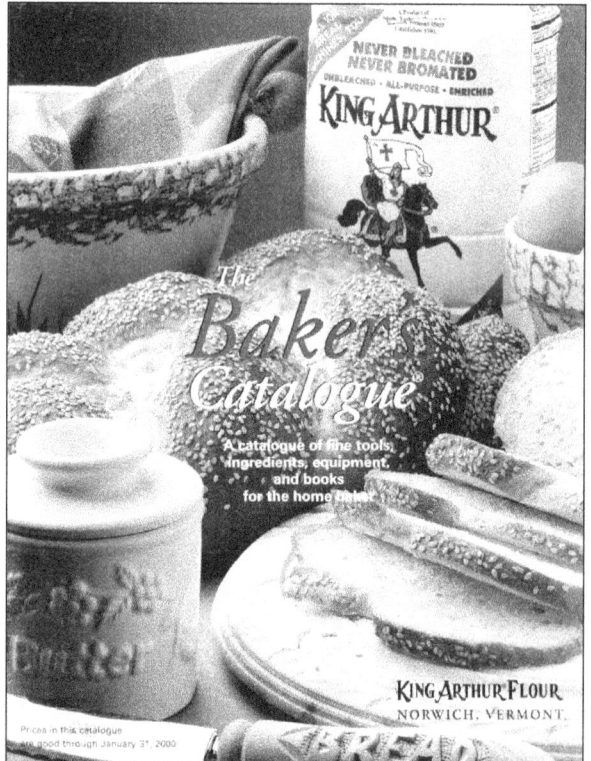

Shown here is the 2000 edition of *The Baker's Catalogue*.

In 2003, *The Baker's Companion* cookbook was published to rave reviews, and it sold more than 75,000 copies in less than a year. It won the prestigious James Beard Award.

TIMELINE

1790: Henry Wood imports flour from England to Boston's Long Wharf, the beginning of the King Arthur Flour Company.

1837: Richard and Company, at 13 Long Wharf, is the earliest known name of the company. The company remains at 13 Long Wharf until 1862, when the water is filled in to create State Street. Without moving, the company address becomes 172 State Street.

1830: The company name changes to Cook & Wood.

1840: The first member of the Sands family, John Low Sands, joins the company as a salesman.

1853: The company name changes to Henry Wood & Company.

1862: The company name changes to Bowker & Edmunds.

1863: The company name changes to James Edmund & Company.

1878: The company name changes to Sands & Fernald.

1881: The company name changes to Sands, Fernald & Sprague.

1885: The company name changes to Sands, Sprague & Taylor.

1888: The company name changes to Sands, Page & Taylor.

1895: The company name changes to Sands, Taylor & Wood, a name that sticks until 1999.

1896: The King Arthur Flour brand is introduced at the Boston Food Fair.

1904: The company moves down the street to the Custom House, at 131 State Street.

1923: The company moves to Somerville, Massachusetts.

1955: The company moves to Cambridge, Massachusetts.

1967: The Wayside Inn gristmill in Sudbury, Massachusetts, is leased to mill King Arthur stone-ground whole-wheat flour.

1976: The company is headquartered in Brighton, Massachusetts.

1978: A warehouse in Andover, Massachusetts, is purchased.

1984: The company moves to Norwich, Vermont.

1990: A 200th anniversary cookbook, *The Baker's Catalogue*, is published for the first time.

1992: King Arthur Flour Baker's Store opens in Norwich, Vermont.

1995: A new 16,600-square-foot timber-frame headquarters, named Camelot, is built in Norwich, Vermont.

1996: The company begins the Employee Stock Ownership Plan.

1998: A new 35,000-square-foot warehouse, named Avalon, is built in Wilder, Vermont, one mile south of the company headquarters.

1999: The company name officially changes to the King Arthur Flour Company.

2004: The company's next cookbook, *The Baker's Companion*, wins the James Beard Award.

www.ingramcontent.com/pod-product-compliance
Lightning Source LLC
Chambersburg PA
CBHW081229190326
41458CB00016B/5723